Tethered Citizens:

Time to Repeal

the Welfare State

Sheldon Richman

ISBN 1-890687-01-4 *(cloth)* — ISBN 1-890687-02-2 *(pbk.)*
Copyright © 2001

The Future of Freedom Foundation
11350 Random Hills Road, Suite 800
Fairfax, Virginia 22030

Library of Congress
Catalog Card Number: 2001-131464

Printed in the United States of America

Cover art by Beth Bowlby

For Jennifer, Emily, and Benjamin

My three top reasons for opposing the welfare state

The more one considers the matter, the clearer it becomes that redistribution is in effect far less a redistribution of free income from the richer to the poorer, as we have imagined, than a redistribution of power from the individual to the state.

— Bertrand de Jouvenel

The state is the great fictitious entity by which everyone seeks to live at the expense of everyone else.

— Frédéric Bastiat

What do we do with it [the budget surplus]? We could give it all back to you and hope that you spend it right.

— President William Jefferson Clinton

Contents

Acknowledgments   *vii*

Preface by Jacob G. Hornberger   *ix*

Foreword by Congressman Ron Paul   *xi*

Introduction by Richard M. Ebeling   *xv*

Chapter 1:
What the Welfare State Really Is 1

Chapter 2:
Didn't We Vote for It? 23

Chapter 3:
How It Started 45

Chapter 4:
The Idea of the Welfare State in America 65

Chapter 5:
What About the Poor? 91

Chapter 6:
Time to Abolish the Welfare State 113

About the Author   141

About the Publisher   143

Index   145

Acknowledgments

Once again Jacob Hornberger has my undying gratitude for his support and encouragement at so many levels. He saw books in me that I had no idea were there. I'd also like to thank Mark Brady, Ralph Raico, Leonard Liggio, Roy Cordato, Richard Ebeling, and Donald Boudreaux for their fruitful comments and suggestions. Elaine Hawley, the librarian at the Institute for Humane Studies' Harper Library, again rendered vital cooperation. Thanks also to Paige Moore and Ronn Neff for their skill in turning a manuscript into a book and to Shirley Kessel for the index.

Preface

It is impossible to overstate the significance of the revolution that took place in the United States in the 1930s during the presidential administration of Franklin D. Roosevelt. Prior to that time, the primary purpose of government in America was to protect people's lives, liberty, and property, which included the rights to freely engage in economic enterprise, to accumulate wealth, and to decide what to do with that wealth. While there certainly had been instances in which government largess had been used to feather the nests of special interests, it was commonly believed that it was morally wrong to use the force of government to take money from one person in order to give it to another person. The advent of the modern-day socialistic welfare state under Franklin Roosevelt fundamentally altered the role of government in America in one fell swoop.

For several years after the Roosevelt revolution, American conservatives challenged the new welfare-state paradigm on both moral and utilitarian grounds. Their arguments were encapsulated in the words of the 19th-century French free-market advocate Frédéric Bastiat, who described the state as "the great fiction through which everybody endeavors to live at the expense of everyone else." It was morally wrong, conservatives argued, for government to plunder one group of citizens for the purpose of distributing the loot to another group of citizens.

Faced with a loss of credibility among the mainstream media and a loss of political power from voters, however, conservatives ultimately threw in the towel and accepted the premises of the FDR revolution. Like other Americans, conservatives today complain incessantly about the inefficiency and ineffectiveness of welfare programs, but their answer is always the same — to call for reform, rather than repeal, of the programs. Today, while conservatives still preach the virtues of private property, free markets, and limited government, they wholeheartedly embrace the welfare-state policies that they know constitute an abandonment of those principles.

Today, it is only the libertarians who strike at the heart of Roosevelt revolution by calling for the repeal, rather than the reform, of every single welfare state program, department, and agency. Our reasons are simple. First, it's morally wrong for the state to take money from a person to whom it belongs in order to give it to a person to whom it does not belong. Second, people cannot be considered free as long as the state has the power to plunder some for the benefit of others. Third, welfare state programs have done a terrible amount damage to the American people, not the least of which is the mindset of government dependency it has engendered among the citizenry.

Two years ago, in his book *Your Money or Your Life: Why We Must Abolish the Income Tax,* Sheldon Richman showed why we should rid ourselves of the primary funding mechanism of the welfare state. With the publication of *Tethered Citizens: Why We Must Abolish the Welfare State,* Richman completes the call for a new revolution in America — a moral, intellectual, political, and economic revolution that would bring an end to political plunder and privilege and restore freedom and limited government to America.

— Jacob G. Hornberger
Founder and President
The Future of Freedom Foundation

Foreword

Sheldon Richman's *Tethered Citizens: Time to Repeal the Welfare State* is precisely the type of scholarly work needed to wake up the American people to the dangers posed by the welfare state. Richman demolishes the popular myth that the welfare state was a natural outgrowth of the Founding Fathers' conception of individual liberty. In fact, the ideology behind the welfare state is a 180-degree turn from the individualism embraced by the Founders. The men who led the American Revolution and drafted the Constitution understood that people flourish best under conditions of freedom — and that a centralized state has neither the legitimate authority nor the competence to care for the needy. Instead, the Founders realized that a state which attempts to provide security will end up destroying both liberty and the economic prosperity necessary to enhance individual security.

In contrast, the theoreticians of the welfare state believe that people are incapable of improving their condition and would ultimately become little more than pawns of the "greedy capitalists" without the support of a wise and benevolent state. Of course, while redistributionism and its nasty cousins — socialism, communism, and fascism — have created many shortages, one thing it has produced in abundance is power-hungry politicians eager to protect the people from the forces of private greed!

In fact, as Richman points out, one of the prime motivations of Bismarck, who created the prototype of the modern welfare state, was to use taxpayer monies to bribe the citizens into supporting his imperial regime. The use of the welfare state to cement popular support for the incumbent government remains intact. As a United States congressman, I regularly see how prevalent the welfare state mentality is among elected officials who use the tool of redistribution as a means of "buying votes" with the taxpayers' own money.

One of the most powerful arguments used by those who would expand the welfare state is that absent government-provided welfare the lives of the poor would be "nasty, brutish and short." Richman demolishes this argument by showing how voluntary charities and organizations, such as friendly societies that devoted themselves to helping those in need, flourished in the days before the welfare state turned charity into a government function. Today, government welfare programs have supplemented the old-style private programs. Many private charities have become seduced by the siren song of taxpayer funding into becoming little more than appendages of the welfare bureaucracy. One of the most disturbing trends of recent years is the attempt by many so-called conservatives to entice the remaining independent charities into government dependency under the guise of expanding access to "faith-based" institutions. Of course, entanglement with the dependency-fostering welfare state will destroy the very attributes that make these institutions effective — freedom from government infiltration and regulation.

While voluntary charities promote self-reliance, government welfare programs foster dependency. In fact, it is in the self-interests of the bureaucrats and politicians who control the welfare state to encourage dependency. After all, when a private organization moves a person off welfare, the organization has fulfilled its mission and proved its worth to donors. In contrast, when people leave government welfare programs, they have deprived federal bureaucrats of power and of a justification for a larger amount of taxpayer funding.

As effective as this book is in showing the harm done by our current welfare policies, it would be a mistake to lump Richman in with those writers who condemn the welfare state's cost and corrosive effects on society in order to build a case for making the welfare state more "efficient." Unlike many policy analysts, Richman does not ignore the fundamental immorality behind the welfare state, which is, after all, built on theft. If it is wrong to rob Peter to pay Paul, how can it be right to levy taxes on Peter to pay Paul?

By tracing the history of the welfare state and detailing how redistributionism damages both the taxpayer and the recipient of government "aid," Sheldon Richman has produced a book that is essential reading for any American wishing to understand how the welfare state is incompatible with constitutional government and a free society. Such understanding is the first step toward reclaiming liberty. For only when the American people fully understand how damaging the welfare state is to both the nation's economy and its moral character will the welfare state join other forms of statism on the ash heap of history.

All lovers of freedom have reason to be grateful to Sheldon Richman for his excellent work and to the Future of Freedom Foundation for publishing it.

— *Congressman Ron Paul*

Introduction

In the twentieth century, practically every form of political and economic collectivism was tried and failed. Socialism, communism, fascism, and Nazism have all been relegated to the dustbin of history. Each promised a freer, most just, and more prosperous society for those who had previously been denied freedom, justice, and wealth by the exploitation and repression of some dominating social, national, or racial group. And each of these variations on the collectivist theme had assured that these good things would come about from a more direct and comprehensive government planning and control of social and economic life by wise and benevolent planners and regulators.

Collectivism's legacy in the aftermath of each of its variations has been social, political, and economic destruction and decay. Tens of millions of people were sacrificed on the altar of remaking the human being into some type of "new man." And the creative efforts of many generations over numerous centuries were destroyed through acts of social engineering or the violence of war.

But in spite of totalitarian collectivism's demise, the ideal of freedom has not fully triumphed in its place. The world is still in the grip of the idea of the interventionist-welfare state. This idea predates modern totalitarian collectivism and indeed was the predominant political-economic system before the emergence of free-market capitalism in the nineteenth century. Mercantilism was the name for the set of economic policies in the seventeenth and eighteenth centuries under which government was assumed to have the responsibility to control and regulate both domestic and international commerce and trade. In England the welfare state idea was instituted in 1601 during the reign of Elizabeth I under what became known as the Poor Laws and which remained in effect and unreformed until 1834. The Poor Laws established the principle that individuals and their families had a right to the financial support of the state, with the funds derived from taxation and distributed to those declared to be eligible through the parishes of the Church of England.

In 1871, Henry Fawcett, one of the last of the great English classical economists, published a book entitled, *Pauperism: Its Causes and Remedies.* Pockets of severe poverty, he explained, had continued to exist in Great Britain during the nineteenth century when the British economy was growing and expanding and providing many in the society with rising standards of living that had never been known before. The main culprit, Fawcett argued, were the Poor Laws, which had created a set of perverse and harmful incentives and attitudes among the very poor the welfare distributions were meant to assist. In Fawcett's own words:

> Men were virtually told that no amount of recklessness, self-indulgence or improvidence would in the slightest degree affect their claim to be maintained at other people's expense. If they married when they had no reasonable chance of being able to maintain a family, they were treated as if they had performed a meritorious act, for the more children they had the greater was the amount of relief obtained. All the most evident teachings of common sense were completely set to naught.... An artificial stimulus was thus given to population.... Population was also fostered by a still more immoral stimulus. A woman obtained from the parish a larger allowance for an illegitimate than for a legitimate child. From one end of the kingdom to the other people were in fact told not only to marry with utter recklessness and let others bear the consequences, but it was also said, especially to the women of the country, the greater is your immorality, the greater will be your pecuniary reward. Can it excite surprise that from such a system we have had handed down to us a vast inheritance of vice and poverty?

And Fawcett pointed out to his English readers that the welfare programs of his day had created dependency "by successive generations of the same family." He reported that a government commission investigating the effects of the Poor Laws found "three gen-

xvi

erations of the same family simultaneously receiving relief." He also pointed out that after a time it was common for those on welfare to begin to believe that they were entitled to it: "The feeling soon became general that pauperism was no disgrace, and the allowance which was obtained from the parish was just as much the rightful property of those who receive it, as the wages of ordinary industry."

Though state-funded welfarism never was completely eliminated in Great Britain in the nineteenth century during the zenith of free-market liberalism, it was greatly reduced with primary responsibility for assistance and support for the less-fortunate and less well-off shifting to private charities and other private alternatives. How successful was the voluntary sector in taking an increasing responsibility for activities? English economist William Stanley Jevons (who was not an advocate of laissez faire), in his 1870 presidential address to the British Association for the Advancement of Science, pointed out: "Could we sum up the amount of aid which is, in one way or another, extended by the upper class to the lower classes, it would be almost of incredible amount, and would probably far exceed the cost of poor law relief."

But Jevons believed that voluntary charity, in this period of supposed Victorian stoneheartedness, had become excessively generous. "It is well known," he said, "that those towns where [private] charitable institutions and charitable people most abound, are precisely those where the helpless poor are most numerous.... The casual paupers have their London season and their country season, following the movements of those on whom they feed. Mr. Goschen and the poor law authorities have of late begun to perceive that all their care in the administration of relief is frustrated by the over-abundant charity of private persons, and religious societies." Jevons, in fact, believed that private charities and charitably funded hospitals should be turned over to state control not because of their niggardliness but because of what he considered their excessive generosity! He wanted to rein in the abundance of private charitable giving, and all at a time before a charitable deduction could be made from one's income-tax liability.

Sheldon Richman correctly points out that the origin of the modern welfare state lies in Imperial Germany in the last decades of the nineteenth century. Fearful that the German Social Democratic Party might win a majority of the seats in the parliament, the German chancellor, Otto von Bismarck, with the support of Kaiser William II, sponsored the passing of a series of welfare programs, including national health insurance, social security, and unemployment insurance. In the 1890s, Bismarck explained his tactical goal to William Dawson, an American historian and Bismarckian sympathizer: "My idea was to bribe the working classes, or shall I say, to win them over, to regard the state as a social institution existing for their sake and interested in their welfare." The welfare state was meant to save the established order-of-things in Imperial Germany from a feared threat from the German democratic socialists by "bribing" workers with a series of interventionist and welfarist policies. The German welfare state became the model and ideal for "progressive" thinkers and policy advocates in the both Great Britain and the United States in the first part of the twentieth century.

Just as the old English Poor Laws reached a crisis point in the early decades of the nineteenth century that led finally to cutbacks and retrenchment and a growth of private-sector charity in Great Britain, the modern welfare states in both North America and western Europe have now reached a crisis point. In the United States, the push has been towards diminishing the incentives for remaining on welfare by threatening a reduction or termination of welfare payments if the welfare recipient does not find gainful employment within a certain period of time or does not meet more carefully drawn criteria for eligibility. And during the period of high economic growth and expanding employment opportunity in the United States during the last half of the 1990s, the welfare rolls around the country have fallen dramatically from a decade earlier.

But nonetheless the bureaucratic and institutional structures of the welfare state continue to exist and function at both the state and federal levels of government in the United States. What is still basically unchallenged is the premise and justification for the government system of welfare. And if the U.S. economy were to experience a significant downturn, the government welfare rolls would no doubt increase once more towards their pre-reform levels.

Furthermore, as long as these government-welfare institutional structures exist, those who man the bureaucracies and the politicians who legislate policy will continue to be tempted to search for ever-new rationales for maintaining and expanding the programs as the means to power and votes. In the following pages, Sheldon Richman not only tells the sad tale of the consequences of the welfare state in America, he also explains the immorality of coerced redistribution of wealth that in fact undermines the proper moral sense in human relationships and weakens the spirit and the capacity for charitable giving to those who may be deserving and in need. And equally important, he outlines the nature of such private charity in a truly free society that eliminates the last vestige of collectivism in our time: welfare paternalism. The future of freedom may well depend up the success to which Sheldon Richman's well-written and insightful analysis helps change the terms of debate over welfare in America.

— Richard M. Ebeling
Vice-President of Academic Affairs
The Future of Freedom Foundation

1

What the Welfare State Really Is

Have you ever stopped to think how tethered you are to government at all levels? As citizens of the United States of America — land of the free, home of the brave — we don't like to think of ourselves as tied to and dependent on government. It clashes with our self-image as free and independent people. But even though skopticism about the efficacy and good intentions of government is higher than in many years, each of us is bound to it in more ways than we can count. We are so used to the tether that we don't feel it any longer. We sometimes even mistake it for freedom.

Government "benefits" are insidious. As the bureaucracy "gives" things away, it inexorably takes something away, a piece of freedom. People see the "benefit," but miss the costs. The administration of William Jefferson Clinton was a perfect lesson in that regard. When he saw a problem, he tried to solve it by inducing people to behave in his prescribed way, often bribing them with their own money if necessary. Clinton's 1999 State of the Union Address was a laundry list of such proposals. Tax credits laden with conditions abounded, but no cuts or repeals. Most illustrative was his United Savings Accounts idea. Americans save too little, he said. Did he propose repealing taxes (such as the Social Security payroll tax) so we might save more? No, we might spend it and not save it. Instead he pledged to open a savings account for each American with $100, then match the contributions we make (with a little extra for low-income people). Such is how a president turns free citizens into tethered citizens.

And there is more than one kind of cost to welfare state programs. There is money cost for the government's handouts, of course. The money has to come from somewhere; nothing is free. But the cost is well hidden in each person's tax bill. Quick: how much are you paying for "free public education"? You don't know. The price is hidden in your property tax and other taxes. But since payment is disconnected from service, people are able to think of the services as free. In fact, they have to pay whether they use the services or not. Parents who send their children to private school pay for education twice.

The money cost of the welfare state has increased horrendously in the twentieth century. Today the federal government spends about $1.8 trillion, more than 20 percent of gross domestic product, an extraordinary amount in peacetime. At least 65 percent involves the transfer of wealth from its producers to nonproducers (rich, middle class, and poor). A tiny fraction of that budget would be required simply to keep the civil peace and defend the territory of the United States.

Here's a sample of where the tax money goes, according to the 2001 budget:

> Education, training, employment, and social services:
> $68 billion.
> Health: $167 billion.
> Medicare: $221 billion.
> Income Security: $260 billion.
> Social Security: $426 billion.
> Veterans' benefits and services: $46 billion.
> Natural resources and environment: $25 billion.
> Transportation: $50 billion.
> Community and regional development: $11 billion.
> General science, space, and technology: $20 billion.
> Agriculture: $9 billion.
> (Source: *U.S. Office of Management and Budget*)

Even if we define "welfare" narrowly, the numbers are astounding. So-called human-resource programs at the federal level cost the taxpayers more than $1.2 trillion in fiscal 2001. (These include education, training, employment, and social services; health; Medicare; income security; Social Security; and veterans' benefits and service.)[1] Social-welfare spending by city, county, state, and the federal governments increased (using 1995 dollars) from $8 billion in 1930 to some $900 billion in 1990, a rise from 1 percent to 13.4 percent of gross national product. The per capita cost rose from $66 to $3,500.[2]

The budget, of course, understates the government's diversion of wealth. The huge regulatory apparatus, state and federal, is a transfer machine, the real size of which never shows up in the federal budget. Yet the costs run into the hundreds of billions of dollars.

The other, more important cost is in terms of lost freedom and independence. When government "gives" away benefits, it makes decisions for the beneficiaries; it assumes control, however subtle. The beneficiaries become less human, because man's distinctive characteristic is the ability, thanks to his rational faculty, to chart his own course. There's nothing humane about the welfare state.

The welfare state is not directed just at "the poor." If that were the case, it would not last long. The middle and upper classes, who pay most of the taxes, would grow weary of giving without getting. So the architects of the welfare state make sure that significant and conspicuous benefits flow to the taxpaying sector. That makes those citizens feel good about the system and thus creates an indispensable consensus for its continuation. That is especially important for the middle class, since that is where so many votes reside.

Look at some of the ways the middle class is bought off by government programs for which they will pay without realizing it: "free" public schooling (which is expanding in the number of hours and services rendered); low-interest college loans and grants; FHA mortgages permitting small down payments for home ownership; subsidized day care; medical care; and unemployment compensation, workman's compensation, Medicare, and Social Security.[3] This is just a short list

Despite appearances, none of those programs is free or without strings. Wherever we turn, we find officers of government promulgating rules, enforcing mandates, requiring information, demanding money, hectoring us about how we live. It has been said that in the first half of the nineteenth century, the typical American citizen could go through his life and — except for the local postmaster — barely see an official of the federal government. Today you can barely get through a day without having contact with power that emanates from Washington, D.C. Throw in state, county, and local officials, and we are virtually surrounded by the "swarms of officers," to use Jefferson's immortal phrase from the Declaration of Independence, that so offended the American Founders.

Considering the proposition to which this country was dedicated — that all people are endowed with certain unalienable rights — this, to put it mildly, should be disturbing.

Disturbing and yet largely unappreciated. How many areas of life are governed by lawmakers and bureaucrats? A multitude, and more all the time. Jefferson hadn't seen anything! Were he to return today, he would not believe his eyes. It was he, after all, who said that government should do no more than keep people from injuring each other and otherwise leave them to their peaceful pursuits. We have come a long way since that was the dominant view in America.

How tethered are you? Let us try to count the ways. (Alas, there is too little room for an exhaustive list.)

When you were a child, the nature of your education was determined not by your parents but by government officials. All the big issues surrounding your schooling were in the hands of politicians and bureaucrats. Your curriculum, including what you learned about government, was determined by government. Your college education may have been at a state-owned institution or subsidized by government through loans or grants, making you dependent on government for a key part of your development. Even if you went to a private college, it was most likely burdened with various requirements related to "civil rights" and "political correctness."

Of course, this is all true of your children's education too. Bureaucrats decide what school they will attend. They tell you when your children will begin school and when they can leave, how many hours a day they will attend, how many days a week, how many weeks a year, how many years. They determine what your child will study and when. They dictate which values are taught or whether the curriculum will be "value-free" (which of course it can't really be).

If you aspire to send your children to college, you will find that federal loans and grants have inflated tuitions, increasing the demand for more federal loans and grants and making it increasingly impossible to attend without them. Education programs are a key to keeping the middle class tethered to government. They give politicians the power to scare people whenever budget and tax cuts are proposed. They only need to ask, do you want your child's college aid reduced?

Since you began making money, you have had to report your income each year to the Internal Revenue Service and to the tax officials in most states.[4] A big part of everything you earn goes to the income-tax collectors even before it reaches your hands. In most states, your retail purchases are taxed. Your real estate is taxed. Sometimes your personal property is taxed. Everything is taxed at some level of government. When you die, what you leave behind will be taxed too.

How you save your money is subject to a web of regulatory offices, from the Treasury Department to the Federal Reserve System to the Securities and Exchange Commission and more. Government regulations dictate how banking services may be provided to you.

The age you could begin earning money, how many hours a day you could work, and under what conditions were decided by government. The minimum wage you could ask of an employer was also set by government. Rules imposed by the U.S. Labor Department, Occupational Safety and Health Administration, and other federal and state agencies take many decisions about your job out of your hands.

Laws favoring labor unions may force you to pay dues to an organization you may have no desire to support. Because of those laws, your relationship with your employer may be intruded on in ways that offend you. Your work conditions may be ridiculously micromanaged by the federal Occupational Safety and Health Administration, lowering your wages and leaving you less money to guard against greater threats to your safety.

If you start your own business, you encounter myriad and onerous rules, requirements, mandates, and taxes. Possibly, they were so onerous you gave up your dream of having your own business. For many kinds of work — from cutting hair and driving a taxi to practicing law and medicine — you are required to pay dearly for a license to practice. Bureaucrats and current practitioners, who have an incentive to limit competition, set the conditions for your entering those jobs. (Yet, somehow, quacks are not a thing of the past.)

Many of the products and services you use are governed by specifications imposed by public officials. Those specifications may bear little or no relationship to what you would choose on your own. Automakers have to meet "fuel-efficiency" and other requirements, which encourage the production of smaller, less-safe cars. Toys can be taken off shelves if the government deems them dangerous. Your toilet and household appliances must satisfy energy and other efficiency requirements. If you need certain medicines, government officials won't let you have them without first paying a high-priced doctor for a prescription. Some medicines and medical devices are forbidden to you altogether if the Food and Drug Ad-

5

ministration isn't satisfied with their safety and effectiveness. Thanks to the FDA, even terminal patients can't get experimental drugs and proven painkillers.

The government, of course, tells you what substances you may and may not ingest for recreation. To enforce these laws it is willing to abuse your civil liberties on an ever-widening scale. To protect you from the scourge of drugs, the government is free to seize property from people never even charged in a crime, to engage in widespread surveillance, to grind financial privacy into dust, to harass people because they fit the profile of a drug dealer. Some antidrug zealots have talked about shooting small airplanes out of the sky because they may be heading back from Latin America. (Of course, they may be carrying a group of buddies heading home from a fishing trip.) Nothing must impede the government in its crusade to keep you safe and sound. (That crusade once included alcohol, of course, the prohibition of which nearly everyone acknowledges was a disaster.) If your right to property and due process have to be compromised, well, so be it. And if you get caught in the crossfire of a black-market gang war, those are the breaks.

Even a legal recreational substance — alcohol — is heavily regulated "for your own good." In some states, it is sold only in government stores. The hours of bars are regulated. You can be arrested for giving your child a sip of wine, even for religious purposes. (My otherwise law-abiding parents broke the law every Friday night of my childhood.)

Your food is inspected by the government. (Yet, somehow, tainted meat and vegetables still make it to the supermarket shelves.) Thus you are falsely lulled into thinking the government keeps you safe. What information appears — and doesn't appear — on food and beverage labels is also the government's domain. Even truthful statements, for example, relating the health benefits of alcohol, cannot be placed on packages without permission.

The government also presumes to take care of you by overseeing your safety in the air, on the rails, on the water, and on the roads. Yet despite its assurances, it cannot keep you safe. It just lulls you into thinking that it can.

The government forces you to support currently retired persons, on the promise that when you retire, other workers will be forced to support you (at a paltry and diminishing "rate of return"). That's called Social Security. On the same promise, you are also forced to pay for the medical care of older people. That's called Medicare. If you are already retired, you may not buy medical care with your own money outside the Medicare system without serious consequences to you and your doctor. If you work, you lose part of your promised Social Security benefits, unlike those from a private pension plan. The fiscal unsoundness of Medicare and Social Security has been much commented on. They will be broke in the not-too-distant future. But even if the systems were sound, have you ever questioned the wisdom of leaving the quality of your retirement years in the hands of bureaucrats and politicians — people who can change the rules at any time and who are not noted for their foresight and wisdom? Can you truly say you are in control of your life if you are not in control of the planning for your later years?

You might own land, but that doesn't mean you control it. How you use it is subject to many laws and regulations. You could buy property as an investment, only to find that when you are ready to retire, you cannot sell or develop it to produce a comfortable income. Perhaps it has been declared a wetland by environmental authorities or determined to be the habitat of an endangered bird, rat, or insect. But don't worry. It's for your own good.

Your plans to build a home or business are also subject to local codes regarding materials, plumbing, electrical equipment, minimum lot size, setbacks, and so on. Officials may deny your building license if you don't submit to extortion of one kind or another. For example, if you want to put up an addition to your building, you may first have to set aside open space or a bicycle path for the public. Zoning laws dictate where you locate a home, business, or religious sanctuary, and how small your lot can be.

Many things that you buy are artificially expensive because government taxes production, limits the supply of foreign-made competitive goods from steel to peanuts, and supports high prices in various ways. You can't buy products from across the border unless the government lets you. Thanks to government-backed agricultural marketing orders, even domestic fruits and vegetables can be barred from grocery shelves if they are smaller or less attractive than standards allow.

You may not know it, but your job might be sustained by barriers to foreign products. If so, you are at the mercy of the caprice of politicians. Trade restrictions may appear to save jobs, but what they actually do is keep people in less-productive work. Free trade encourages people to specialize where they have a comparative advantage. Protectionism interferes with that process, holding down incomes and tethering workers to the government's trade and labor policies.

7

If you want to hire or otherwise associate with someone who happens to have been born across the U.S. border, the immigration authorities will object. The civil rights authorities watch your hiring, selling, and renting policies. If they don't like the statistical profile of your staff, you could be in for a major legal war. You are not trusted to decide with whom you will deal.

If you want to gamble, the government will tell you where and under what conditions you may do so. Or it might forbid your gambling altogether. Government lotteries are fine; private numbers operations, with better odds, are not. Private casinos are permitted, if it suits the officials' plans. Government knows better. If you win, be prepared to turn over part of the prize to the taxman, if it isn't withheld before you see it.

If you want to do the more respectable kind of "risk-taking," on the various stock, commodity, and derivatives markets, you again face a complex tangle of rules that undermine the efficient workings of markets and reduce your return. If you have innocently obtained something undefined called "inside information" and profit from it, watch out! You might have committed a crime.

And speaking of money, let's not forget that government manages the monetary system. While its power to run the system has been eroded by the increasing sophistication of global markets, people over the years have suffered inflations, recessions, and depressions thanks to the government's wise management.

Sending first-class mail means dealing with the government's post office — the paradigm inefficient bureaucracy, which is why it needs to bar competition to continue in existence. If you try to use an overnight service for purposes the government does not deem "urgent," you'll still owe the post office for the postage you tried to avoid.

Mail isn't the only business the government is in. Amtrak and Conrail put the government in the passenger and freight rail business. It has its hands all over the electric power industry. It controls space exploration. It parcels out the airwaves.

Government of course forces you to engage in charitable activities. Welfare programs, the provision of money and services to people in "poverty," deprive you of the freedom to decide how you will show compassion toward your fellow citizens. In the bargain, government creates or aggravates social problems, such as illegitimacy and crime, which inevitably haunt productive, law-abiding citizens.

As if all that isn't enough, there are people who would like you to be tethered to the state even more. They would have the government finance and dictate the terms of all medical care — a cradle-to-grave tether that would have life-and-death consequences for everyone. After all, if government is the purchaser (with tax money) of medical services, it will have the power to say who gets what services. It can't work any other way. Child daycare is another area where government threatens a takeover. The advocates of activist government, moreover, would like to see private property regulated even more than it is now. The environment is the most popular pretext for the subversion of property rights.

These government activities are for your welfare. Or that's what the champions of those programs say. Welcome to the welfare state.

There is an increasing belief that government programs don't work well and are too costly. The schools neglect academics while they pursue a dubious political and cultural agenda. Social Security is going broke. Business and agricultural subsidies favor the well-connected and wealthy. And so on. But even if they "worked," or cost less, the welfare state's programs would be objectionable because they are the means by which government exerts control over its citizens. This sort of "kindness" kills.

If citizens have rights, that control is bad. It dehumanizes. It defies and defiles the original spirit of America.

How egregious is the tethering? Social Security, the crown jewel of the welfare state, has already been mentioned, but let's look at it more closely. The first fact about Social Security is that it is not an insurance plan. Money taken from workers is not invested; it is given to retirees, who spend it. Future benefits depend on future taxes. Strictly speaking, there is no return on the money taxed. (This has economywide consequences, since what would be savings is consumed.)

The worker is entirely passive in the matter. Government determines the payroll-tax rate, the formula for calculating benefits, and the minimum retirement age. It can change the rules at any time it can get away with it politically. Over the years Congress has increased benefits, but it has also raised taxes. While earlier retirees collected more in benefits than they paid in taxes, later ones have seen their net benefits approach zero. Future retirees may get a negative "return." The worker has no enforceable contract with the government and thus cannot sue for breach if the rules are changed. He is, to be blunt, at the mercy of politicians and bureaucrats. His retirement ultimately rests on political caprice.

The rules are likely to be changed in the next several years because Social Security's fictitious trust fund is dry and early in this century the revenue from the payroll tax will be insufficient to cover the benefits paid out. (That will happen for demographic reasons. Eventually, when the baby boomers retire, there will be only two workers for each retiree; in the past there were as many as forty-two workers for each retiree.) Congress may try to "fix" the system by delaying retirement, cutting benefits, or raising taxes. Any of those measures would expose the system's victimization of its alleged beneficiaries by changing the rules unilaterally.[5]

The tethering can also be seen in the one-size-fits-all nature of the system. People must take what they are given by the government, no questions asked. But people, and groups, are different, so the system isn't quite the same for everyone. For example, white men on average live longer than black men. Thus, white men will draw benefits longer than black men. Yet since both groups are subject to the same tax policies, black men get an even worse deal than white men.

Now contrast this absurd system with a private pension. Without Social Security, workers would tailor retirement-savings plans to their own requirements and preferences. They would be free to contract for investment services, reflecting their own taste for risk and retirement, and those with whom they contract would be freely accepting enforceable legal obligations. Each individual would be in the driver's seat. Government could not force him to save more or less than he wishes. It could not change his benefits. It could not set his retirement age. The tether would be cut.

Social Security gives power to government. Its repeal would give power to individuals.

The story is similar with Medicare. Since the program's cost has predictably gotten out of control, the government now sets the price for medical services for the elderly. When government sets prices below the level the free market would set, it creates shortages. In this case, doctors don't want to treat elderly patients if they are insufficiently reimbursed for their labor. If the elderly offer to pay directly for the medical care, they are in violation of the Medicare regulations — and the doctor will be penalized. The health of the elderly is at the mercy of government policy.

The tether of America's democratic welfare state is not usually the heavy-handed tyranny of totalitarian and authoritarian states. It is subtler and more insidious. But our humane, moderate welfare state is immoral and damaging nonetheless.

In the 1830s Alexis de Tocqueville had the prescience to see the dangers that American democracy held for its people. In volume 2, part 4, of *Democracy in America*, Tocqueville's chapter 6 is titled "What Sort of Despotism Democratic Nations Have to Fear."[6] It is remarkably instructive.

Reflecting on the tyranny that plagued the people of antiquity, Tocqueville decided that the citizens of a modern democracy faced a despotism of a different character. "It would be more widespread and milder," he wrote; "it would degrade men rather than torment them." He believed that in "an age of education and equality," government power could be more pervasive yet less harsh than in previous times. "I do not expect their leaders to be tyrants," Tocqueville wrote, "but rather schoolmasters." He expected that as people became centered on their own lives and families, they would not notice that over them "stands an immense, protective power which is alone responsible for securing their enjoyment and watching over their fate."

What does this government do to its people? Tocqueville says "it only tries to keep them in perpetual childhood." It does so by providing security and necessities, assuming responsibility for their concerns, managing their work, and more. "It gladly works for their happiness but wants to be the sole agent and judge of it."

Tocqueville's foresight is so keen and his exposition so exquisite, that he is worth quoting at length.

> Thus it [government] makes the exercise of free choice less useful and rarer, restricts the activity of free will within a narrower compass, and little by little robs each citizen of the proper use of his own faculties....
>
> Having thus taken each citizen in turn in its powerful grasp and shaped him to its will, government then extends its embrace to include the whole of society. It covers the whole of social life with a network of petty, complicated rules that are both minute and uniform, through which even men of the greatest originality and the most vigorous temperament cannot force their heads above the crowd. It does not break men's will, but softens, bends, and guides it; it seldom enjoins, but often inhibits, action; it does not destroy anything, but prevents much being born; it is not at all tyrannical, but it hinders, restrains, enervates, stifles, and stultifies so much that in the end each nation is no more than a flock of timid and hardworking animals with the government as its shepherd.

I have always thought that this brand of orderly, gentle,

peaceful slavery which I have just described could be combined, more easily than is generally supposed, with some of the external forms of freedom, and that there is a possibility of its getting itself established even under the shadow of the sovereignty of the people.

Tocqueville went on to say that the people wanted two contradictory things — guidance and freedom — and imagined they could have both. The people "console themselves for being under schoolmasters by thinking that they have chosen them themselves. Each individual lets them put the collar on, for he sees that it is not a person, or a class of persons, but society itself which holds the end of the chain."

America perhaps has not gone fully down the path Tocqueville warned of. But it has gone a long way. The era of big government is not nearly over, the slogans of cynical politicians notwithstanding.

Tocqueville understood that democratic tyranny is insidious. It is possible that some welfare-state programs, looked at in isolation, have benefited you. But it is misleading to look at them in isolation. All together they have cumulative moral and economic effects that must not be ignored or underrated. The system binds you and makes you dependent on power. It encourages you to look at government as your protector, implying that, first, you are too frail to look after yourself and, second, that a free, self-regulating society would be full of peril and without its own forms of protection. And unless you are immune from the welfare-state ideology, the handouts also tend to make you concerned about cutbacks in government spending. Most people don't want to lose their government benefits. They have developed a stake in their own continued dependency. They have developed the fateful "entitlement" mentality.

The advocates of the welfare state emphasize the alleged benefits of their programs. The government protects you from bad decisions, bad people, bad products. They play down the flip side: control. But if government officials, no matter how sincere, are to care for and protect you, they must be able to control you. How can it be otherwise? When statists called for laws requiring motorcyclists to wear helmets, they argued that as long as the government is ready to pay for the medical care and disability benefits of cyclists with head injuries, it was justified in mandating the use of helmets. That argument has a logic to it. He who pays the piper calls the tune.

Everyone understands that caring for a child requires control.

12

To abdicate control is considered child neglect. The same applies to government and citizen, but there is a big difference. Tethered citizens are not children. They are adults with the right to govern their own lives. The advocates of absolute monarchy used to compare the king to the father and the subjects to his children. The American colonists fought a revolution to overthrow that idea on these shores. But the idea never died. It went more or less dormant, then came back, modernized and democratized, with a vengeance.

Government care and government control always go together. Subsidies entail regulation. Nothing is given away. You must obey. As the U.S. Supreme Court said in the landmark 1941 *Wickard v. Filburn* case, when it refused to stop the intrusive regulation of a subsidized farmer, "It is hardly lack of due process for the Government to regulate that which it subsidizes."[7] If you have other ideas for how to save for retirement, you still must participate in the government's system. If you wish to make your own decision about food and drugs, too bad. If you want to educate your children free from all government standards and testing, sorry, you're out of luck.

Care requires control, which requires obedience. That is a major reason that governments always control education. What better way to instill obedience in future citizens than by controlling their education and teaching them early on that government is benign and must be obeyed?[8] Paternalism, kind or cruel, slowly suffocates the human essence. It is a corrosive and coercive bargain: security for liberty. Ben Franklin saw that was a bad deal more than two centuries ago. But it is even worse than it sounds. It's like one of those pacts with the devil, in which a greedy man accepts material security in exchange for his soul, and ends up with neither. With the welfare state, you don't get real security in return for liberty. You get strangers making decisions for you. Who are those strangers? Can they be competent to make decisions for you? Do they know your unique circumstances, requirements, and aspirations? If not, you don't get security. You get only a false sense of security, which is worse than no security at all.

The links to the welfare state are thus tethers, limiting your right to decide how to shape your life to the fullest extent possible. Only human beings confront the question *What should I do with my life?* And to the extent that the government supplies the answer, it makes us less human.

But shouldn't government protect us from the ups and downs of life? In its attempt to do so, it inevitably creates many of those downs. To carry out paternalism, it must interfere with the work-

13

ings of the market economy, that is, the spontaneously coordinated productive activities that people engage in daily. And when it does that, it makes us poorer than we would have been. Resources and effort are diverted to purposes chosen not by the people, who are in a better position to know what they want and need, but by policy-makers, who can only claim to know better. Things that people want are not produced, at least not in the quantity they wish. Society is poorer than it would have been. Such impoverishment necessarily hurts the most vulnerable in society. Thus, the people who seem to be most in need of government paternalism will be its chief victims. The rich and well-connected will probably do well under any arrangement.

The advocates of the welfare state have offered a false alternative: security provided by government versus hazard. They don't know, or don't want you to know, that a free society can provide a reasonable degree of security without a loss of liberty.

As an idea, the welfare state is nearly dead. The economic argument mounted against welfarism — by Mises, Hayek, Friedman, Hazlitt — is awesome and unanswered. (The moral argument, with an exception or two, has been weaker.) Political philosophers still try to construct elaborate intellectual defenses for activist government, but they read like glib exercises aimed at justifying power over people's peaceful decisions. For example, some writers have argued that activist government is necessary to save people from social norms and expectations that they haven't chosen.[9] Others argue that government measures are needed to ensure that the differences among people serve the interests of the least "advantaged" in society.[10] Still others believe government must guarantee that the "strong" fulfill their moral duties to the "weak."[11] And some writers have promoted some notion of equality of condition as an ideal.[12] All of these defenses of government activism, however well-meaning, are calls for the use of force against people who have behaved peacefully and productively. Citizens who have committed no crime of violence or fraud against others would be forced to surrender some of their belongings to others. By what right? Because someone else is in need? "Need makes right" is no more defensible than "might makes right." Only right makes right.

While dead in intellectual terms, the welfare state is not dead in practical terms. It is faltering. It is unstable. Its budgets are in deficit. It is searching for ways to cut back on its extravagance without alienating constituents. It is doing more things "off budget," through mandates on the private sector. But it is not yet on the coroner's slab, toe tag in place. The welfare state will be able to muddle along indefinitely unless the moral challenge to it is as formidable as the economic challenge.

This book will examine the theory and practice of the welfare state. There is a library full of excellent books on the fatal moral and economic flaws of welfarism.[13] There is a large literature dissecting particular welfare state programs and demonstrating how interest-group politics causes government spending and regulation to grow. This book will not attempt to cover that ground. Rather, it will consider various political, historical, and philosophical topics that have not gotten as much attention as others have. Therefore, it is intended to complement the work of other authors.

What is the welfare state exactly? As Jack Douglas has written in his book *The Myth of the Welfare State,* no state ever claimed to be opposed to the welfare of its citizens.[14] The highly limited national government of the early United States was dedicated to the "general welfare." Concern with welfare per se does not distinguish one state from another. What counts is how welfare is conceived.

Ludwig von Mises saw how the welfare statists skillfully used the language to obscure this fact and anesthetize the opposition.

> They intentionally employ a term the generally accepted connotation of which precludes any opposition. No decent man likes to be so rash as to raise objections against the realization of welfare. In arrogating to themselves the exclusive right to call their own program the program of welfare, the welfare propagandists want to triumph by means of a cheap logical trick. They want to render their ideas safe against criticism by attributing to them an appellation which is cherished by everybody. Their terminology already implies that all opponents are ill-intentioned scoundrels eager to foster their selfish interests to the prejudice of the majority of good people.[15]

Douglas notes that the Founders of the United States understood that the general welfare lies in the protection of individual liberty because liberty — freedom from physical force — is indispensable for the pursuit of each person's own welfare and happiness. It is often argued that the presence of the term "general welfare" in the preamble and Article I of the U.S. Constitution accords plenary paternalistic power to the federal government. That idea is directly contradicted by James Madison, the acknowledged author of the Constitution: "With respect to the words 'general welfare,' I

15

have always regarded them as qualified by the detail of powers con-
nected with them. To take them in a literal and unlimited sense
would be a metamorphosis of the Constitution into a character which
there is a host of proofs was not contemplated by its creators."[16] In
other words, the phrase "general welfare" cannot be used to twist a
charter of limited, specified, and delegated powers into a grant of
limitless powers.

The Founders' ideas were based on the notion that the general
interest is not separate from or in conflict with the interests of individuals. Society consists of individuals, and its good must be seen
in terms of their good. In contrast, the typical welfare state pretends
that the general welfare and general interest are something other
than the good of all individuals. In its rhetoric, welfarism is collectivist. In practice, of course, its policies subordinate some individuals to others in the name of the general welfare.

As used in this book the term "welfare state" refers to government that exceeds the scope traditionally favored by classical liberals. It signifies a state that does more than maintain civil peace with
courts and police and protect against foreign invasion with armed
forces. In theory, a welfare state presumes to guarantee the well-
being of society through the provision of a broad range of services
and subsidies, including poor relief, administration of pensions,
provision of schooling, and guidance of the economy. Under that
mandate, almost any service or subsidy could be deemed appropriate.

The form of governance we call the "welfare state" has gone by
other names, including the mixed economy, state socialism, national
socialism (Nazism), corporativism, industrial democracy, and fascism. These terms apply to activist states of varying dimensions.
The welfare state is distinguished from socialism and communism
by the absence of complete formal government ownership of the
means of production, though the state may own selected firms and
industries.

Welfare states are engines of paternalistic wealth transfers.
Theoretically, they rearrange property ostensibly for the good of society. Most of what the U.S. government does fits that description.
The motivation does not need to be the transfer of wealth, though
often it is. Objective effects are what count. The welfare system, or
public assistance, has the explicit purpose of transferring wealth.
Transfer is both the end and the means. The same holds for Social
Security. Drug prohibition, on the other hand, does not have the
stated goal of transferring wealth. Its goal is the suppression of drug

16

use. But in objective effect, it is a massive wealth-transfer program. Huge sums of money move every year from taxpayers to politicians, law enforcement officials, drug rehabilitation experts, and others. Many programs fit that mold.

"Welfare" will be used in its broadest sense to include all government transfers. It will include handouts for the middle class and wealthy as well as the poor. It will also include "corporate welfare." If we were to look only at benefits for the poor, we would end up with an inadequate examination of the welfare state. What used to be called "relief" is but a small part of the welfare, or transfer, state. Its social consequences are serious, but relief to the middle class and corporate world has serious consequences too.

Transfers can be indirect. Take protectionism, for example. The purpose of protectionism is to shelter selected domestic producers from foreign competition. One way it does so is by taxing imports. The money raised by tariffs, of course, goes to the treasury for general purposes. But that is only part of the transfer that occurs. Protectionism also transfers money from buyers of imports to the protected domestic businesses. Tariffs raise the price of imports to consumers, permitting domestic manufacturers to raise their prices higher than if they faced lower-priced foreign competition. When consumers buy fewer imports and more domestic products, the result is similar to a direct subsidy from the treasury.

Import quotas work similarly. Americans pay about twice the world price for sugar because importing foreign sugar is artificially restricted by quotas. Congress could have simply appropriated money to sugar producers. But providing the subsidy by means of a quota is more artful and harder for the average citizen to detect.

The government has an endless number of indirect ways to transfer wealth. As the free-market advocates Henry Hazlitt (in the twentieth century) and Frédéric Bastiat (in the nineteenth) taught, to understand government we must look at the unseen, secondary effects of its policies. There is a coercive transfer in virtually every government act. Someone loses out. However the state channels money into favored hands, it must thereby deprive others of something they would have had. That is the real cost of the transfer. To look at only one side of the transaction is to create a grossly distorted picture of reality. It would be like a balance sheet without a liability column. There are those who have an interest in seeing reality that way.

When government action is examined, we have a strong temptation to venture into the treacherous waters of motivation. We want to know the *real* reason a particular program was established. Was the motive good or bad? Is the advocate of a program a humanitarian or a mean spirit? People often seem satisfied if they conclude the motive was good. The substance of the program is less important than the sponsor's state of mind.

Here we will not be concerned with motives or intentions. Rather, our focus will be on objective phenomena: what the welfare state does. Speculation about motives is always tricky. Who can say what is in a person's mind or heart? Here people will be taken at face value.

Policies have objective consequences, and it is unimportant what motivated those who enacted them. Imagine the welfare statist's bête noir, a rich and miserly curmudgeon who despises the poor and concludes (because of his economic ignorance) that the way to keep the poor down is for the government to pursue laissez-faire policies. His intentions tell us nothing about the objective consequences of the policies he espouses. An economist who wants to see the poor achieve higher living standards would advocate the same policies. The curmudgeon's motive must not be allowed to taint the idea, which ought to be judged on its merits using the best economic and political theories available. Conversely, someone who says he wants to help the poor through government action cannot avoid a hardheaded evaluation of his policies simply because his intentions sound compassionate.

This is not to say that motives are unimportant, only that the identification of motives does not take the place of substantive analysis. As noted, programs tether the general population — not just poor people — to government and even to a particular political party or politician. Thus, political leaders will push for programs because they create or strengthen the allegiance of a constituency. There is strong evidence that Medicare was enacted in 1965 at least in part, for that reason. The economist Charlotte Twight writes that the administration of Lyndon Johnson and its allies in the Congress "knew that Medicare would create a vast new public dependence on the federal government for financial security in old age, continuing the pattern set by Social Security in 1935." She notes that the policymakers knew that once the program began, all the pressure would be toward expanding it. She goes further and demonstrates that the policymakers knew *they* would benefit by passing the legislation. House majority leader Carl B. Albert of Oklahoma said on the floor that the bill "will serve well those of us who support it, politically and otherwise, through the years."[17]

18

A similar calculation occurred with Social Security three decades earlier. Ironically, President Franklin Roosevelt insisted on making the employees' contribution explicit in order to create a public stake in the program. Roosevelt said, "We put those payroll contributions there so as to give the contributors a legal, moral, and political right to collect their pensions and their unemployment benefits. With those taxes in there, no damn politician can ever scrap my social security program."[18] (Of course, no legal right was created.)

But again, consequences, not motives, are what count. Even if politicians were not aware that their welfare-state policies would create dependency and political dividends, those policies would be every bit as defective morally and economically. Intentions count for nothing when it comes to the evaluation policies. The law of unintended consequences sees to that.

This book aims to persuade the intelligent general reader that the welfare state is a snare. In objective consequence, it lures people in, entangles them in apparent benefits, and imposes controls allegedly for their own good. While it seems to bestow benefits on them, it compromises their independence and integrity. It inculcates an "I'd better get mine before someone else gets it" mentality. It makes them receivers of stolen goods because all transfers originate in theft from the taxpayers.

It is hoped that by the end, readers will see that the welfare state, though it promises security and stability, actually inhibits the achievement of those values while robbing individuals of their liberty and autonomy, key elements of our Western inheritance. If they then withdraw their support and acquiescence, vocally question the system, and embrace freedom, we will have made progress toward the liberty that is the American people's birthright.

The people legitimate the welfare state by their tacit acceptance. If the welfare state is to be abolished, that acceptance must be withdrawn. Objectively speaking, the welfare state is illegitimate. But doesn't it gain legitimacy by being the product of democratic decision-making? That is the first claim to which we will turn.

Notes

[1] Traditional welfare, Aid to Families with Dependent Children, was replaced in 1997 with a system of block discretionary grants to the states. More on this in chapter 5.

[2] See David Kelley, *A Life of One's Own: Individual Rights and the Welfare State* (Washington, D.C.: Cato Institute, 1998), p. 4. Kelley's figures come from the *Statistical Abstract of the United States, 1997.*

[3] Thanks to my friend and colleague Beth Hoffman for reminding me of these programs.

[4] See Sheldon Richman, *Your Money or Your Life: Why We Must Abolish the Income Tax* (Fairfax, Va.: Future of Freedom Foundation, 1998).

[5] See James L. Payne, "Social Security Doesn't Work Any More," *The American Enterprise,* January/February 1997, pp. 41–44.

[6] Alexis de Tocqueville, *Democracy in America,* trans. George Lawrence, ed. J. P. Mayer (1848; New York: Perennial Library/Harper & Row, 1988), pp. 690–95. The subsequent quotes are from this section.

[7] Quoted in Jeffrey R. Snyder, "Unrestrained Appetites, Unlimited Government," *The Freeman: Ideas on Liberty,* May 1998, pp. 285–89.

[8] See Richman, *Separating School and State: How to Liberate America's Families* (Fairfax, Va.: Future of Freedom Foundation, 1994).

[9] See Cass Sunstein, *Free Markets and Social Justice* (New York: Oxford University Press, 1997), in which the author calls for expanded government power to protect individual autonomy.

[10] See John Rawls, *A Theory of Justice* (Cambridge, Mass.: Harvard University Press, 1971).

[11] See Robert E. Goodin, *Reasons for Welfare: The Political Theory of the Welfare State* (Princeton, N.J.: Princeton University Press, 1988).

[12] This can take several forms. See Edward Bellamy, *Looking Backward: 2000–1887,* ed. John L. Thomas (1888; Cambridge, Mass.: Harvard University Press, 1967). Also see Mickey Kaus, *The End of Equality* (New York: New Republic Books, 1992).

[13] The latest is Kelley.

[14] Jack D. Douglas, *The Myth of the Welfare State* (New Bruns-

wick, N.J.: Transaction Publishers, 1989).

[15] Ludwig von Mises, *Human Action: A Treatise on Economics,* 3rd rev. ed. (Chicago: Henry Regnery Company, 1966), p. 834.

[16] Quoted in James Dorn, "Madison's Constitutional Political Economy: Principles for a Liberal Order," *Constitutional Political Economy* 2, no. 2 (1991): 181.

[17] The quotations are from Charlotte Twight, "Medicare's Origin: The Economics and Politics of Dependency," *Cato Journal* 16, (Winter 1997): 334–35.

[18] Quoted in William E. Leuchtenburg, *Franklin D. Roosevelt and the New Deal, 1932–1940* (New York: Harper Torchbooks, 1963), p. 133.

2

Didn't We Vote for It?

Can we democratically vote ourselves into the welfare state? And if that's what happened, how can anyone fairly complain about it? That is likely to be the response of many people to objections to the monstrosity we are tethered to. We live in a democracy, it will be said. We the people voted for the leaders who in turn voted for the programs that constitute the welfare state. If you voted in the minority, that's a risk of living in democracy. If you don't like the outcome, the only thing to do is keep voting or run for office.

To examine this defense of the welfare state, we must put democracy itself under powerful microscope. We must look, in the words of William Mitchell and Randy Simmons, at the "unromantic side of democracy."[1] It isn't pretty.

Before we plunge in, this should be said: if democracy merely means choosing officeholders by vote, then it is surely preferable to choosing them by violence. But that is a very low standard. It's like saying someone is better than Hitler. We should set the bar higher.

When someone endorses democracy, he is most likely saying more than simply that officeholders should be chosen by vote. But we can't be sure how much more he is saying. That vagueness is what gets us into trouble.

Very few people are full democrats, or majoritarians. That is, almost no one wants the people to vote on what religion, if any, we should all follow; what careers we should pursue; whether we should own pets; how we should live generally. In other words, everyone has at least a tacit notion of a zone of autonomy that is, or should be, beyond democratic reach. It is a cliché to say that in our democracy, the majority rules but the rights of the minority are protected. Like a cheap sweater, it falls apart at the merest tug on the loose thread. Either it means the majority votes only on things that do not affect anyone's rights or it is a contradiction in terms. The former is not usually what democrats have in mind. Majorities can be tyrannical. Tocqueville saw the danger when he visited the young United States. "My greatest complaint against democratic government as organized in the United States," he wrote, "is not, as many Europeans make out, its weakness, but rather its irresistible strength. What I find most repulsive in America is not the extreme freedom reigning there but the shortage of guarantees against tyranny."[2]

Obviously, it is not enough to say that you support democracy. Crucial is what you think the voting public ought to be able to decide. *Who* rules is not as important as *which* rules. In other words, what officeholders may do is more important than the precise method of how they are selected.

An older school of American conservatism used to say, "This isn't a democracy; it's a republic." There was wisdom in that. (Today's conservatives, epitomized by Robert Bork and Justice Antonin Scalia, are unabashed majoritarians.) The U.S. Constitution is full of devices to limit the power of government and the democratic process. The first words of the revered Bill of Rights are "Congress shall make no law." That is a limit on what the people may do. Their representatives may not restrict religion, speech, assembly, and petition of the government for redress of grievances. It is an absolute prohibition. (It is not observed any longer; but that's what the document says.) The Second Amendment says the people's right to own guns "shall not be abridged." That's another limit on what the people collectively may do. The Constitution proper grants only a few powers to the federal government ("few and defined," Madison said). It is full of anti-majoritarian devices. The president is elected by an Electoral College, not directly; it is possible for the winner to lose the popular vote — as has happened four times in American history, most recently in 2000. The president has the constitutional power to veto bills passed by a majority of the people's representatives in Congress, which needs a supermajority to override. The Framers were obviously not majoritarians.

Going beyond the Constitution, we can see immense moral problems with democracy. First, something isn't right simply because a majority of voters say so. Most democrats believe "the people" delegate rights to their government representatives, which they then exercise legitimately. But surely we can't delegate what we don't first possess. I don't have the right, for example, to compel you to give me 12 percent of your income on the promise that when you retire I will provide you a pension (financed by similar extractions from others). If I don't have that right and you don't have that right, we can hardly delegate it to the government. So how did Social Security, the crown jewel of the welfare state, become enacted? In general, if I don't have the right to compel you to do something you don't wish to do, I also don't have the right to get a bunch of people together to put the question to a vote — even if we let you have a vote. A lynch mob might be called direct democracy, but it was usually a murderous band as well.

The economist and author Walter Williams says that if consensual market transactions are like seduction, then involuntary political transactions are like rape. And democracy is like gang rape. That is the unromantic side of democracy, indeed.

It's evident that the key to democracy is that one group imposes its will on another. Let's see how that's so. In a representative democracy, such as the United States, citizens typically do not vote on particular issues but for members of legislative bodies. Their "representatives" then vote on legislation and policies to govern their particular jurisdictions. Obviously, all those votes entail losers. Citizens who voted for the losing candidates are bound nonetheless by the winners' decisions, and citizens whose representatives are on the losing side of legislative votes are likewise bound by the decisions of the representatives who prevail. (For now, we'll skip the added complication that representatives often break campaign promises.)

A classic defense of the system was made in an essay by Anthony Downs, who wrote,

> The basic arguments in favor of simple majority rule rest upon the premise that every voter should have equal weight with every other voter. Hence, if disagreement occurs but action cannot be postponed until unanimity is reached, *it is better for more voters to tell fewer what to do than vice versa.* The only practical arrangement to accomplish this is simple majority rule. Any rule requiring more than a simple majority for a passage of an act allows a minority to prevent action by the majority thus giving the voter of each member of the minority *more weight* than the voter of each member of the majority.[3]

The late Italian liberal jurist and political scientist Bruno Leoni, however, demolished Downs's argument that majority rule assumes that "every voter should have equal weight with every other voter." He pointed out that in fact "we give much more 'weight' to each voter ranking on the [winning] side ... than to each ranking on the [losing] side.... The fact that we cannot possibly foresee who will belong to the majority does not change the picture much."[4] In other words, Leoni argued, when a bare majority prevails in an electorate of 100, 51 have the weight of 100 and 49 the weight of zero.[5]

The problem, of course, is that the legislative process is a winner-take-all matter. That fact refutes the various attempts of political scientists to liken the process to the marketplace. As Leoni noted:

> Only voters ranking in winning majorities (if for instance the voting rule is by majority) are comparable to people who operate on the market. Those people ranking in losing minorities are not comparable with even the weakest operators on the market, who at least under the divisibility of goods (which is the most frequent case) can always find something to choose and to get, provided they pay the price.[6]

In the legislative process, Leoni argued, you either get what you asked for (theoretically) or you get nothing. "Even worse, you get something that you do not want and you have to pay for it just as if you had wanted it."[7] That makes the legislative process, he added, more like the battlefield than the marketplace. In an imaginative application of the Ludwig von Mises's criticism of socialism, Leoni also analogized the legislative representative to the central economic planner; by the very nature of their systems, both are cut off from information that is critical to the jobs they are theoretically doing because the spontaneous processes that produce that information are squelched. As he put it:

> No solemn titles, no pompous ceremonies, no enthusiasm on the part of applauding masses can conceal the crude fact that both the legislators and directors of a centralized economy are only particular individuals like you and me, ignorant of 99 percent of what is going on around them as far as the real transactions, agreements, attitudes, feelings, and convictions of people are concerned.[8]

The civics books portray democracy as a sacred process of collective choice. We join together, cast our votes, and choose our leaders. In his last presidential address to Congress, Abraham Lincoln said, "The most reliable indication of public purpose in this country is derived through our popular elections."[9] On the Wednesday after the Tuesday after the first Monday in November of each election year, editorial writers throughout the land wax rhapsodic about the almost mystical nature of the people's communion and decision-making. But we have cause to doubt Mr. Lincoln and the editorial writers.

A collective is not a real entity. It does not act or *choose*. It does not have a scale of values or any of the other elements of choice. Collective action and choice are metaphors, which we must not take literally. Collective choice can be reduced to the vote choices made by individuals. But we must be aware that the constraints and incentives facing individuals when making political choices differ dramatically from those they face when making other kinds of choices.

Think of your last trip to the supermarket. You had your money in your pocket, and you were there to select items that you and your family would consume. Each choice you made was decisive. In other words, presented with a choice between Wheaties and Cheerios, whichever you chose is the one you got. Every time you selected an item, you made an implicit estimation that it would better satisfy you than anything else you could spend the money on. If you chose Wheaties, you expected more satisfaction from that product than from Cheerios or cheese or frozen peas or a night out bowling or saving the money. The cost of your selection was your second highest-ranking preference, which you passed up in making your choice. Economists call that the "opportunity cost."

In the supermarket, moreover, you constructed a basket of items precisely to your liking. You were not stuck with package deals put together by someone else. You didn't face a choice between Wheaties/milk/frozen peas and Wheaties/yogurt/frozen corn. That's a good thing for those of us who want Wheaties/milk/frozen corn. We don't get stuck with something we don't want in order to get something we do want. A store that required that would find itself with few customers. (Of course, at times products are bundled; but if that does not meet consumer approval, competitors will reap the business.)

One final point about supermarkets: if you get home and find that the bags contain a different selection of products from the one you made, you have recourse. The supermarket will rectify the error, because it knows you will shop elsewhere if it doesn't. As a last resort, the legal system exists to resolve your grievance.

In those circumstances, where the chooser confronts the costs and benefits, and his act is decisive, we can expect choices to accurately reflect preferences. Preferences are *demonstrated* by the act of choosing. We have no other clue to them. When it comes to divining preferences, what people do is more telling than what they say.

Because supermarkets and markets in general are organized that way, they do a good job of satisfying consumers. Our preferences are communicated unambiguously to merchants and entrepreneurs, and they strive to make supply match demand. When we wake up in the morning, we are reasonably certain that the stores will have milk and the other items we want and need. Markets work, which is why they are taken for granted.

The political system is sometimes compared to a marketplace, with votes as the currency and government services as the items bought. But that is misleading. The differences between market choices and political choices are monumental. They appear to start off on the same foot. Individuals express choices: in the market for products and services, at the polls for candidates and, in referendums, for policies.

But while individuals make choices in the political realm, the choices are tallied up to determine the outcome. That is a serious difference. When you choose Wheaties, you get Wheaties — end of story. But if you vote for Jones, you don't necessarily get Jones. Enough other people must also choose Jones before you get what you want; they might vote for Smith. In fact, your one vote means little in the scheme of things. In most elections, the chance of a tie is minuscule. The outcome will be the same whether you vote or not. There may be rational reasons for voting, but expecting to determine the outcome is not one of them. This point upsets many people, but it is mere arithmetic.

In 1960, the presidential election was extremely close by historical standards. It is often used to rebut the claim that one vote doesn't count. How close was that election? If one vote had switched from John Kennedy to Richard Nixon in half the precincts, Nixon would have won. Fine. Do you have a vote in half the precincts? More likely you only have one vote in one precinct. So you could not have changed the outcome of that election, no matter what you did.

Of course, if enough people had changed their votes or had voted for Nixon instead of staying home, the result would have been different. But that is outside the range of choice for any person. We must look at this from the perspective of the individual. Each person controls only whether or not to cast *his* vote and if so, to vote for X rather than Y. That decision is unlikely to affect the decisions others make (certainly not enough others). But even if you could determine the choice of enough other people and affect the outcome, your staying home would still make no difference. One vote is as a grain of sand on the beach. One more or less is insignificant.

When we vote we do not face the same opportunity cost that we face at the supermarket. Recall that in the supermarket, when you choose Wheaties, you forgo Cheerios (or whatever ranks No. 2). What opportunity is forgone when you vote for Smith over Jones? Since you are unlikely to determine the result of the election, you cannot be said to forgo Jones as the winner; a vote for Jones wouldn't put him in office. All you forgo by voting for Smith is *voting* for Jones. That's probably not much of a cost.

If Smith supports big spending programs that would require higher taxes, there may be a later cost attached to the election of Smith. But keep in mind, first, that the cost will be spread over the entire population and not imposed on the single voter, and second, the voter's choice is not decisive. The cost of the candidate's proposals are not terribly relevant to how people vote. That explains why elections are more about sentiment and image than substance.

There is another obvious difference between elections and shopping. In elections, we are confronted with package deals. Each candidate has a collection of positions covering hundreds of issues. You may like some of his positions, and dislike others. But you can't choose among them. It's all or nothing. Moreover, if after the election, your candidate changes his mind about an issue (or reveals himself as having misled the voters), you are out of luck. You can't have the election staged again. You can't sue. You can't go to a competing system.

Thus, Geoffrey Brennan and Loren Lomasky sum up the case: except in the unlikely case of tie-breaking, "the voter receives one or other bundle [of 'services'] irrespective of the preference he himself exhibits. In that sense, it is misleading to describe electoral 'choice' as a choice between *a* and *b*: It is, rather a choice between expressing a preference for *a* and expressing a preference for *b*.... The opportunity cost of voting for *a* is simply not voting for *b*, with no implications for the electoral outcome at all."[10]

The answer to the question "Didn't we choose the welfare state fair and square?" is: No, the mechanism for making political choices has intrinsic defects that permit us to doubt that it creates results reflective of what individuals would choose if they faced the benefits and costs directly. We may have a welfare state, but that doesn't mean we as a society want a welfare state.

Let's look more closely at the issue of the constraints on choice. We've noted that when an individual goes shopping, he faces constraints. Products have prices he will have to pay, and he has a specific income. He has to make choices within those constraints. In the political realm, we've seen that he will pay only a fraction of the total cost of government programs. When he votes, he is actually voting to force the rest of society to pay for what he wants. Under those conditions, people will vote for all kinds of things they would reject under other circumstances. Lots of people would want a Porsche if someone else would pay for it. Since everyone votes on the same basis — knowing they won't pay the full cost of their choices — the system is skewed toward expansion of government.

"The divorce of costs from benefits not only induces a favor-seeking motive in each citizen," Mitchell and Simmons write, "but in the long run also turns democracy into a vast celebration of the repeal of what Milton Friedman called TANSTAAFL — 'there ain't no such thing as a free lunch.'"[11] That is why Frédéric Bastiat called the state the fiction by which everyone tries to live at everyone else's expense.

David Friedman compares the political system to a hundred people sitting in a circle, each with a hundred pennies in his pocket. A politician takes a cent from each and gives one person 50 cents. "After a hundred rounds, everyone is a hundred cents poorer, fifty cents richer, and happy."[12]

Whatever simile you pick, it is clear that democracy, as a system for choosing how to spend money, leaves much to be desired.

The system is also skewed by "logrolling," trading votes. It happens in legislatures all the time. Representative Smith votes for Representative Jones's bill in return for Jones's voting for Smith's bill. An implicit form of logrolling occurs when citizens vote for candidates some of whose positions they don't like. With logrolling, bills are passed and candidates picked that don't faithfully reflect people's preferences. Again, the separation of costs and benefits distorts the decision-making process.[13]

Logrolling can lead to bizarre outcomes. Mitchell and Simmons offer the case of three citizens who vote on two projects: a jail and a school. Each voter estimates the cost and benefits of each project to himself. If voter A opposes each project, voter B supports the jail but opposes the school, and voter C supports the school but opposes the jail, each project would lose in an individual up-or-down vote, 2–1. But if the voters logroll, both projects would be approved. Voters B and C would agree to support each other's pet project and outvote A on each. B and C would force A to help pay for the projects — and his money loss could be larger than their money gain. (Since valuation is personal and immeasurable, we cannot compare satisfaction and dissatisfaction, or pain and pleasure.) Known as a "deadweight loss," that phenomenon is common in government transfers.[14]

Another problem is known as "rational ignorance." A person is rationally ignorant anytime he decides not to obtain knowledge because the benefits are not worth the cost. We make such decisions all the time. Time is scarce, and we can't try to know everything. The political system encourages rational ignorance. Most voters have no incentive to invest time studying all the issues in an election and the biographies of the candidates. Remember, one vote is not decisive. If a voter believes his effort will have no effect on the outcome, he probably will not be motivated to give up other valued things to acquire knowledge about complex issues. Any benefits are probably going to be small to any given voter anyway.

The result is that most voters will have highly limited information about candidates, enough to give them a good or bad sense about the candidates. Most of that information will be received passively, provided by the candidates themselves and the news media.

How ironic that democracy is touted as the system that draws on the wisdom of the people! By its nature, it encourages the mass of voters to be ignorant. Since politicians know this, they pitch their message to an essentially ignorant populace. That's why election rhetoric is often emotional and vague. Candidates try to set a mood without really saying anything. "Political communication is rarely conducive to rational or efficient allocation of scarce resources," Mitchell and Simmons write.[15]

A huge literature on the paradoxes of voting has grown up over the years. These paradoxes don't usually make it into the civics textbooks. But voting can lead to counterintuitive outcomes, as we saw with the jail-and-school case above. Mitchell and Simmons provide another case, this one in which each of three voters ranks three options A, B, and C, in a different order: ABC, BCA, CAB. If a vote is taken on all three options at once, there will be no winner. But if the options are paired, then the winner will be determined purely by the order in which they are voted on. If the first vote is A versus B, A will win. But if it is A versus C, A will lose. Under those circum-

31

stances, how can we say that the people expressed their preferences and got what they wanted? Something is wrong if the *order* of the vote is decisive. An element of caprice resides at the heart of the system.[16]

Democracy suffers from another big problem as well, which stems from rational ignorance. The system is dominated by special interests. Until now we've assumed that in a democracy, majorities rule. But in fact, well-organized numerical minorities actually call the shots. They do so because the benefits of most government programs are concentrated on a small group of citizens, while the costs are dispersed thinly among the entire taxpaying population. This has two implications: the beneficiaries, each of whom stands to profit a great deal, have an incentive to invest money to create and protect programs; and the rest of the people, each of whom will pay only a small amount per program, have little incentive to oppose those programs or even to know what is going on. Advantage special interests.

A large group in which each member stands to gain little from collective action is prone to the classic free-rider problem. Each member has an incentive to let others do the work. Thus, little gets done. But a tightly organized interest group, in which each member anticipates a large payoff, is less likely to suffer the problem, especially if its political activity is tied to other benefits. For example, the farmers' organization ties its lobbying services to insurance.

The paradigm is the federal sugar program. In a country where sugar consumers far outnumber sugar producers, why does the government keep sugar prices artificially high? That same question can be asked about any number of products and commodities. Why don't the consumers outvote the producers? Standard theory of majority rule cannot resolve the paradox.

The sugar program includes strict quotas on foreign sugar. It is intended to benefit American sugar producers by letting them charge prices higher than the free market would set. (Americans sometimes pay double the world price.) It also benefits corn producers and at least one food processor, Archer Daniels Midland. How? Expensive sugar induces food producers who use sugar, such as soft-drink makers, to use cheaper high-fructose corn syrup instead. That pleases the corn growers and ADM, which turns corn into sweetener. Enough other Americans use real sugar to make the program worthwhile for the sugar producers.

Even though the overall cost of the program is large, the price is small for any individual consumer. If he could compute the additional amount he has to pay because of the program, it would most likely seem too small to justify active opposition. Most people are busy making a living and raising their families. The opportunity costs of organizing a campaign against the sugar program would outweigh the benefits even if there was a good chance the program could be abolished. A fully informed citizen would most likely shrug his shoulders with regret and a sense of futility. That is the effect of dispersed costs.

Of course, most citizens are not fully informed — they are rationally ignorant. They don't know they are paying more for sugar than they should have to. And even if they did, they probably wouldn't know why. (They'd probably blame the greed of the free market.)

While the expense to any individual is small, the total cost for all citizens is huge. That reverses the incentives for the small group on the receiving end of the program because those large benefits are divided among the few beneficiaries. Since each member of the group stands to gain a great deal, it is worth his time to actively lobby for the program, or more precisely, to pay dues to a trade association that will set up shop in Washington, D.C., and look after his interests full-time. That is the effect of concentrated benefits.

It is no mystery, then, that special interests prevail over the vast majority of citizens.[17] Most of us have too little to gain materially from trying to stop individual welfare state programs. Maybe that's what Thomas Jefferson had in mind when he said, "The natural progress of things is for liberty to yield and government to gain ground."[18]

Thus, while democracy in theory is the rule of the majority, in practice, it is the rule of minorities. Democratic government in the real world is far different from the one portrayed in textbooks. The electoral and legislative processes, rather than forums for the people to express their will and to look after their collective needs, is more like a bazaar, where interest groups bid on claims to the taxpayers' money. The people who pay most of the bill aren't even there. H. L. Mencken, one of the keenest observers of America, made perhaps his most perceptive remark of all when he wrote in 1936 that "government is a broker in pillage, and every election is a sort of advance auction sale of stolen goods."[19] There is political science in a nutshell. Everything else is commentary.

The houses of Congress in Washington, D.C., (like the state legislatures) are vast political trading floors where interest groups enter bids on programs to serve their members. The programs, of course, are paid for by the mass of unorganized citizens, who, as noted, have neither the information nor the incentive to travel to Washington to object. This is a vast system of lawful plunder, to use Frédéric Bastiat's memorable phrase.[20] The bidding is not open and obvious. Subtlety is the rule. This is where the campaign finance system enters. Well-organized industrial, labor, and other interest groups give money to candidates who are then beholden to their benefactors. They repay, directly or indirectly, in tax dollars.

Politicians play the role of brokers and facilitators, responding to the demands of interest groups. They can also be initiators, origi- nating ideas for programs that will benefit interest groups in order to win support and contributions. There's no better example than the U.S. government's prototype welfare program, the Civil War pen- sion system. Chapter 4 will go into detail, but suffice it here to say that what began as a military pension program for disabled Union veterans expanded into a vast machinery to produce political sup- port for the postbellum Republican Party. Politicians quickly learned the value of handing out money.[21]

The economist Fred McChesney has shown that giving out goodies is only half the story. Politicians often float ideas for gov- ernment action — a tax or a regulation, say — that would hurt an interest group, fully prepared to withdraw it in return for money and support. None dare call it extortion.[22]

(The solution to these problems is not, as many propose, re- strictions on campaign finance, which would amount to abridgment of free speech. Rather, the solution is to drastically scale back the scope of government. If it has no favors to sell, no one will try to buy them.)

Considering the goodies to be won there, it is no surprise that Washington is an interest-group mecca. Here's how journalist Jona- than Rauch, sees it:

> By definition, government's power to solve problems comes from its ability to reassign resources, whether by taxing, spend- ing, regulating, or simply passing laws. But that very ability energizes countless investors and entrepreneurs and ordinary Americans to go digging for gold by lobbying government. In time, a whole industry — large, sophisticated, professionalized, and to a considerable extent self-serving — energizes and then assumes a life of its own. That industry is a drain on the pro- ductive economy, and there appears to be no natural limit to its growth. As it grows, the steady accumulation of subsidies

and benefits, each defended in perpetuity by a professional interest group, calcifies the government.[23]

Rauch has it right, except for his belief that government actually solves problems and that the calcification of government is a drawback. Would that the calcification were more complete! But he correctly points out that all the talent assembled in Washington, if the government were not in the transfer business, would be producing things instead of lobbying. The things not produced are part of the dead-weight loss of the welfare state.

Rauch indicates the expansion of the welfare-transfer state through the growth in interest groups located in Washington. In the 1920s the District of Columbia telephone book listed some 400 lobbies. By 1950, the number was 2,000. Rauch notes the symbolism in the fact that in 1987 the Baha'i faith, which forbids political activity, opened an office for lobbying. A great deal of money is spent seeking transfers and defending against transfers.[24]

Politicians, of course, do more than serve interest groups. They must get reelected; so they do high-profile things that are apparently good for their general constituencies. But any benefits are outweighed by the tax bill for all the special programs. Take away the special-interest service and little is left. (Any real benefits would most likely have been provided by entrepreneurs in the free market.)

This perverse process should give pause to people who want government to help the "needy." Given logrolling and the advantages of interest groups, the government is not likely to remain a benefactor for the poor alone. Its expansion is inevitable. No matter how much the poor might get in direct benefits, they will lose more in indirect costs, such as stifled production, high prices, and fewer employment opportunities.

As if the system weren't impervious enough to scrutiny, the people in charge have many other ways to keep the taxpayers from finding out what is going on. They are masters at obfuscation. Even a highly motivated citizen oblivious to expense would have a difficult time keeping informed. Legislation can run hundreds, thousands, of pages, full of technical legislatese. Consequential law changes can be buried in omnibus bills. Members of Congress often don't read the bills or know fully what they are voting for. Moreover, much legislation leaves the details to regulatory agencies, an unconstitutional abdication and delegation of authority if there ever was one. No member of Congress can know what the outcome of that kind of legislation will be. If a citizen later complains, his congressman can say, "I didn't vote for that; the regulators did it."[25] It's known as "plausible deniability."

Some transfers are so indirect that most people never know they are happening. The sugar program, as noted, transfers money from consumers through the circuitous route of import quotas. Government helps dairy producers by supporting prices, that is, promising to buy products at above-market prices. Why sell to consumers at market prices if government will pay more?

One of the great acts of obfuscation is Social Security. That program was discussed in the last chapter. Here, let's concentrate on one aspect, the employer "contribution." Workers are led to believe that their employers pay half the tax. That makes the system appear cheaper than it really is. In fact, the employer cannot really contribute. As the old saying goes, businesses don't pay taxes; they collect them. Anything an employer appears to pay is really part of the worker's compensation. The entire package of cash wages, non-cash benefits, and taxes (Social Security, Medicare, unemployment insurance, workman's compensation) constitutes the cost of hiring a worker. Employers don't pay workers more than they can contribute to production. Without Social Security, most if not all that cash would be paid to the worker. The market sets pay levels. If the government commands employers to pay into Social Security on behalf of their workers, cash compensation will be reduced or more work will be demanded of them. The appearance of an employer contribution is a clever act of deception and obfuscation.[26]

The nominal employer contribution was just one device used by Franklin Roosevelt's administration to mislead the American public about Social Security. As late as 1934, Americans opposed a compulsory government pension. To dissolve that opposition, Roosevelt, his advisors, and congressional allies systematically employed legislative and public relations techniques to make Social Security appear to be something other than what it was. Those techniques included dishonestly portraying Social Security as an actuarially sound insurance plan complete with personal accounts and tying the program to measures, such as ad hoc assistance to the elderly, that the public supported. The result was passage of a program that Americans would have opposed had it been offered in a straightforward manner. Once Social Security was in place, the political dynamics were all in favor of its permanency and, indeeed, expansion.[27]

Medicare was similarly shrouded from public understanding

from the start. As the economist Charlotte Twight has written, "History shows that Medicare did not and could not achieve passage without the misrepresentation, cost concealment, tying, and incrementalism to which its supporters ultimately resorted.... By tying Medicare to a 7 percent increase in Social Security benefits, proceeding incrementally, narrowing the bill's coverage, misrepresenting its content, concealing its costs, and using countless other transaction-cost-increasing strategies ... government supporters of Medicare were able to achieve their objectives. These same tools, so instrumental in passing Medicare, today continue to serve those who seek further increases in federal control over U.S. health care."[28]

Another form of deception is deficit financing, or government borrowing. Since it obviates the need for politicians to seek tax increases in the short run, it fools citizens (for a while) into thinking that government is cheaper than it really is. Deficit financing is one of many examples of how the political system favors the short run over the long run — ironically, because big-government advocates often fault the free market for being too focused on the short run in the quest for profits. That is specious. It is government, not the private sector, that shortens the time horizon. Business people are always concerned with future value; politicians are concerned with reelection.[29]

Intentional or not, obfuscation and abdication keep the citizen at bay. The shroud protects the beneficiaries. And the taxpayer keeps on paying.

Here's an example. In 1996 there was much ado about welfare reform. Republicans were on record wanting to make drastic changes summed up by the word "workfare." President Clinton promised to end welfare "as we know it." After some wrangling and vetoing, a bill was signed. The New Deal-era Aid to Dependent Children (later, Aid to Families with Dependent Children) was abolished. Welfare as an entitlement was no more. Control was shifted to the fifty states, with Washington providing money and setting a few conditions, among them: welfare recipients had to find jobs within two years and could remain on the rolls no more than five years. The impression was left that this would save the taxpayers lots of money. Welfare statists wrung their hands. A centerpiece of the welfare state was ostensibly being dismantled. Was it? Not quite.

Contrary to the headlines, the Congressional Budget Office's own projections showed an increase in total welfare spending until 2002. The increase will hit $110 billion.[30] True, many people have left the welfare rolls and taken jobs. But government finances daycare and health care. A year after the "reform" took effect, Clinton proposed expanding Medicare and greater government regulation of daycare and child health care. To quote the late Congressman Sonny Bono, "the beat goes on."

How could people have such a wrong impression? It is nearly impossible for an average, busy American citizen to get a handle on the subject. There are upwards of 80 different major welfare programs and more than 160 job-training programs. Perhaps there are more. No one really knows.[31] Reading the budget isn't much help; you'd have to know what you're looking for. And who has time anyway?

So who's watching things if most Americans are not able to? Answer: Those with the biggest stake in the system — the welfare industry. The fox is guarding the chickens. "Welfare today is an enormous industry," writes James Payne, "much larger than the defense establishment, or the tobacco industry, or chemical companies. It supports over 700,000 social workers, 420 schools of social work, thousands of special interest groups, nonprofit organizations, and commercial firms, and some 43 million beneficiaries. Day in and day out, welfare leaders work to expand their industry."[32] They do so by providing a good portion of the propaganda about welfare that is received by members of Congress and the news media. The dice are loaded.

The obfuscation makes its way into the history books. A typical example is government meat inspection, a classic "service" of the welfare state. We all "know" how government got into meat inspection during the Progressive Era, because we learned it in public schools. (Most private schools aren't much different on this.) Americans in the nineteenth century were routinely eating diseased meat. (Don't ask how the population grew and life expectancy increased.) Then early in the twentieth century, Upton Sinclair, a caring socialist novelist, wrote *The Jungle* about the terribly unsanitary conditions at the Chicago stockyards. That prompted a public outcry and demands for government protection, which were fulfilled by decent political leaders.

One problem: it didn't happen that way. There was no critical health problem and no public outcry. Sinclair intended his book to draw attention to the workers' allegedly bad conditions, not the unwholesomeness of meat. Moreover, as he said, "the Federal inspection of meat was, historically, established at the packers' request; ... it is maintained and paid for by the people of the United States for the benefit of the packers."[33]

The historian Gabriel Kolko confirms that meat inspection came at the behest of the meatpackers as much as anyone else and writes that it began long before Sinclair published his novel. A major reason the packers wanted inspection was to assuage fears in the European markets that American meat was tainted. (Europe had its own protectionist rules.) Federal inspection was a way to have the taxpayers foot the bill for saving Europe for the American packers.[34]

Government inspection had domestic public-relations benefits also. As the big packer J. Ogden Armour said, "This government inspection thus becomes an important adjunct of the packer's business from two viewpoints. It puts the stamp of legitimacy and honesty upon the packer's product and so is to him a necessity. To the public it is *insurance* against the sale of diseased meat."[35] But of course the public was doing fine before government inspection. But inspection would tend to hurt small packers more than large ones, which could more easily afford to comply with bureaucratic rules.

In the states, local butcher interests feared the rise of large packers that, because of refrigerated railroad cars and economies of scale, challenged the butchers in their own markets. Local interests were able to get their state politicians to pass protectionist inspection legislation to raise the Chicago packers' prices. That gave the large packers another reason to favor federal inspection: they could control one regulatory agency in Washington more easily than they could control many state agencies. Kolko comments that "the big packers were warm friends of regulation, especially when it primarily affected their innumerable small competitors."[36]

There are similar stories behind the other government ventures into regulation of industry. We are taught it was all for the benefit of consumers and the result of the democratic process. But at the time, it was usually only industry interests that lobbied for intervention.[37]

Business was not the only party to originate economic intervention. Local and national politicians saw opportunities for gain and exploited them. As Eldon Eisenach observed:

> National business corporations and railroads were systematically blackmailed and fleeced by state and local governments exercising their police powers to protect small-producer capitalists and local realty interests. The party organizations would, however, for the right price, arrange favorable environments across jurisdictional boundaries to create economies of scale in production and marketing.[38]

The dishonest nature of the democratic welfare state has far-reaching consequences. For one, it determines who prospers in politics by rewarding those with the skills appropriate to the process and penalizing those who lack such skills. This is the welfare state's version of the survival of the fittest.

In *The Road to Serfdom* F. A. Hayek included a chapter titled "Why the Worst Get on Top." Advocates of government economic planning, he wrote, were unjustified in believing that the ugly brutality of Nazi Germany and fascist Italy were purely the result of bad people's holding dictatorial power. Hayek argued that "humane" dictatorship is not to be expected because a system that concentrates vast powers in one man or group necessarily puts a premium on ruthlessness and violence. People without the appropriate skills will not advance. Fascism wouldn't have produced a Martin Van Buren or a Grover Cleveland.[39]

By the same token, the democratic welfare state selects leaders who exhibit skills appropriate to its characteristic features. It rewards the skills of winning and staying in office, or what Alexander Hamilton in Federalist No. 68 called "talents for low intrigue, and the little arts of popularity."[40] But what does it take to win a majority of voters, the median voters? As we've seen, in light of rational ignorance, it takes skill in image-making, demagoguery, crafty rhetoric, and evocativeness. Those are not the skills that the textbooks would lead us to believe are relevant to governing. But clearly, the system tends to select people with campaigning, rather than governing, skills.

Take the case of Ronald Reagan, dubbed the Great Communicator. The impression he gave was that he was determined to cut the size of government. By the end of his two terms, most people probably think that is what he did. But he did not. The federal government consumed about the same portion of our wealth as it did when he entered office. Some tax rates were cut, but others were raised, particularly the Social Security tax, which was hiked seven out of eight years. Overall tax revenues increased dramatically. There was apparently more downsizing of government in the Clinton years than in the Reagan years. Yet few would believe it.

The upshot is that given the nature of democracy, it is meaningless to say that we the people chose the welfare state we have. It was the piecemeal result of political ambition and brokering, special-interest bidding, and chicanery, fueled by phony crises and misdirected compassion. Bismarck knew of what he spoke when he reputedly said that the people should not see how statutes and sausages are made — an appropriate note on which to end, since Bismarck is the subject of the next chapter.

Notes

[1] See William C. Mitchell and Randy T. Simmons, *Beyond Politics: Markets, Welfare, and the Failure of Bureaucracy* (Boulder, Colo.: Westview Press, 1994), especially chapter 3.

[2] Alexis de Tocqueville, *Democracy in America,* trans. George Lawrence, ed. J. P. Mayer (1848; New York: Perennial Library/ Harper & Row, 1988), p. 253.

[3] Anthony Downs, *In Defense of Majority Voting* (Chicago: University of Chicago, 1960), quoted in Bruno Leoni, *Freedom and the Law,* expanded 3rd ed. (Indianapolis, Ind.: Liberty Press, 1991), p. 237.

[4] Leoni, p. 237.

[5] Leoni agreed that simple majority rule is consistent with "strongly organized minorities" imposing their will. He finds proposals for supermajority rule no better. Ibid., p. 242 ff. See James Buchanan and Gordon Tullock, *The Calculus of Consent* (Ann Arbor, Mich.: University of Michigan Press, 1962).

[6] Leoni, p. 235.

[7] Ibid.

[8] Ibid., p. 23; see also pp. 20–23, 112–32.

[9] Mario M. Cuomo and Harold Holzer, eds., *Lincoln on Democracy* (New York: A Cornelia and Michael Bessie Book/HarperCollins Publishers, 1990), p. 337.

[10] Geoffrey Brennan and Loren Lomasky, *Democracy & Decision: The Pure Theory of Electoral Preference* (Cambridge, Mass.: Cambridge University Press, 1993), p. 23.

[11] Mitchell and Simmons, p. 70.

[12] Quoted in ibid.

[13] Mitchell and Simmons discuss these and related issues in ibid., pp. 41–83.

[14] Ibid., pp. 71–72.

[15] Ibid., p. 73.

[16] Ibid., p. 78.

[17] On the problem of organization, see Mancur Olson, *The Logic of Collective Action* (Cambridge, Mass.: Harvard University Press, 1982).

[18] Thomas Jefferson, Letter to E. Carrington, 1788; quoted in *A New Dictionary of Quotations on Historical Principles from Ancient*

and Modern Sources, ed. H. L. Mencken (1942; New York: Alfred A. Knopf, 1982), p. 482.

[19] H. L. Mencken, "Roosevelt and Alf," in H. L. Mencken, *A Carnival of Buncombe,* ed. Malcolm Moos (Baltimore: Johns Hopkins Press, 1956), p. 325.

[20] Frédéric Bastiat, *The Law* (1850; Irvington-on-Hudson, N.Y.: Foundation for Economic Education, 1998), p. 7 ff.

[21] Theda Skocpol, *Protecting Soldiers and Mothers* (Cambridge, Mass.: Belknap Press of Harvard University Press, 1992), pp. 1–151.

[22] Fred S. McChesney, *Money for Nothing: Politicians, Rent Extraction and Political Extortion* (Cambridge, Mass.: Harvard University Press, 1997) and "High Plains Drifters: Politicians' Lucrative Protection Racket," *The Freeman: Ideas on Liberty,* January 1998, pp. 4–9.

[23] Jonathan Rauch, *Demosclerosis: The Silent Killer of American Government* (New York: New York Times Books, 1994), p. 17.

[24] Ibid., p. 39.

[25] For an example of how big changes can be almost secretly imposed, see Claire Wolfe, "A Number, Not a Name: Big Government by Stealth," *The Freeman: Ideas on Liberty,* May 1998, pp. 298–303.

[26] In response to an employment-tax increase, an employer doesn't simply cut wages. But he may cancel or reduce future increases, or make smaller capital investments, which would mean lower productivity and lower wages in the future.

[27] See Charlotte Twight, "Channeling Ideological Change: The Political Economy of Dependence on Government," *Kyklos* 46 (1993): 497–527. On the bogus nature of the Social Security Trust Fund, see John Attarian, "The Myth of the Social Security 'Trust Fund,'" *Ideas on Liberty,* March 2000, pp. 17–21.

[28] Charlotte Twight, "Medicare's Origin: The Economics and Politics of Dependency," *Cato Journal* 16 (Winter 1997): 309, 335.

[29] Mitchell and Simmons, pp. 73–74.

[30] See the excellent account, James L. Payne, "Welfare 'Cuts'?" *The American Enterprise,* November/December 1997, p. 39. See also Payne's *Overcoming Welfare: Expecting More from the Poor and from Ourselves* (New York: Basic Books, 1998) and "Why the War on Poverty Failed," *The Freeman: Ideas on Liberty,* January 1999, pp. 6–10.

[31] Payne, "Welfare 'Cuts'?" p. 39.

[32] Ibid. Payne notes that the courts are also helpful at expanding the reach of welfare programs.

[33] Quoted in Gabriel Kolko, *The Triumph of Conservatism: A Reinterpretation of American History, 1900–1916* (New York: The Free Press, 1963), p. 103.

[34] Ibid., p. 98. See E. C. Pasour Jr., "We Can Do Better than Government Inspection of Meat," *The Freeman: Ideas on Liberty,* May 1998, which draws on Gary D. Libecap, "The Rise of the Chicago Packers, and the Origins of Meat Inspection and Antitrust," *Economic Inquiry*, April 1992, pp. 242–62. Also see Lawrence W. Reed, "Of Meat and Myth," *The Freeman: Ideas on Liberty,* November 1994, pp. 600–602.

[35] Quoted in Kolko, p. 102. Emphasis in the original.

[36] Ibid., p. 107.

[37] See Kolko's story of the Pure Food and Drug Act, ibid., pp. 110 ff.

[38] Eldon J. Eisenach, *The Lost Promise of Progressivism* (Lawrence, Kansas: University Press of Kansas, 1994), p. 15.

[39] F. A. Hayek, *The Road to Serfdom* (Chicago: University of Chicago Press, 1944), pp. 134–52.

[40] Hamilton thought that those superficial capacities might prevail in a single state, but not in the Union as a whole.

3

How It Started

The welfare state has probably existed in some form for as long as there has been government. Government as we know it originated through conquest rather than social contract. And since the rulers always constitute a much smaller group than the ruled, those who sought to govern long-term undoubtedly found it necessary to buy the support of key constituencies that presented a potential threat to their rule. They paid for that support through confiscation of others; with time, they learned the value of finding methods of transferring wealth — taxation — that permitted the victims to continue producing. (At an earlier stage, the conquerors killed and pillaged but that did not produce wealth long-term.) Victims of taxation themselves were eventually provided benefits in order to give them a stake in the system — without a stake they might resist and deprive the rulers of the fruits of conquest. That entire process is the germ of the welfare state.[1]

It should not be surprising that political governance typically takes the form of a quid pro quo. A ruler who demands allegiance and revenue from a group is likely to be more persuasive if he promises benefits in return. Rule by violence alone is costly; violence provokes resistance, and it's hard to keep good employees. So the evolution of an elaborate system of carrots and sticks is entirely understandable. Under feudalism, for example, the lord of the manor extended protection to his serfs in return for their service. In time, the carrots took a variety of forms: cash subsidies, economic regulations on competitors, discriminatory taxes, franchises, and other ways to bestow favors. Under mercantilism, the crown granted monopolies and other protection against foreign and domestic competition in return for loyalty and revenue. The state dictated nearly all aspects of production. The system's underlying principle was that the welfare of the nation, and the sovereign of course, depended on a growing hoard of gold.[2] We have already seen how the state's power to distribute benefits turns a nation into a special-interest bazaar.

While the carrots typically went to the well-heeled and well-connected, help specifically for the poor was also common from the earliest times. In Elizabethan England, with the secularization of the idea of poverty in the late sixteenth century, poor laws were established embodying "the principle of a legal, compulsory, secular, national system of relief."[3] Those laws endured in some form until England's formal welfare state succeeded them after World War II. The historian Gertrude Himmelfarb points out that the poor laws helped give England the reputation as a country with a compassionate public policy.[4] Relief was administered locally and financed through a tax on households. Almshouses were built to hold the aged and sick. Along with alms came controls and impositions, although it is unclear whether they were the purpose of the relief system. Work was provided for the able-bodied poor. Beggars were punished or imprisoned.[5] In the nineteenth century, England set up workhouses for the poor under a system called "indoor relief."[6] But, as Himmelfarb points out, the nascent welfare state was not only for the poor. Driven later by the Fabians (gradualist democratic socialists), the British welfare state made general provision of old-age pensions and other insurance, as well as other services.[7]

The welfare state in England was a multipartisan affair. The Tory party and even the (classical) liberals played a part in building the system. Tory Prime Minister Benjamin Disraeli favored legislation intended to help workers.[8] Harold Macmillan, a Conservative prime minister, said, "Toryism has always been a form of paternal socialism."[9] Earlier, Lord Acton, the great classical liberal, saw "a latent Socialism in the Gladstonian philosophy."[10] Gladstone, of course, was regarded as a great (classical) liberal prime minister in nineteenth-century England. Yet he gave England death duties on landed estates, a labor department, inspection and regulation of factories, the eight-hour day for railway workers, and workman's compensation.[11]

Yet future prime ministers David Lloyd George and Winston Churchill may be regarded as the architects of Britain's modern welfare state. While president of the board of trade beginning in 1908, Churchill, first a Conservative, then a Liberal, then again a

Conservative, said he favored "a big slice of Bismarckism" to provide "a certain measure of security and safety against hazards and misfortunes."[12] At this time Lloyd George, who had seen Bismarck's welfare state up close, was chancellor of the exchequer and proposed a social-insurance scheme funded by land and income taxes. The system was adopted in 1910 after being thwarted by the House of Lords.

The deep roots of the welfare state are not to be found in England or even Sweden, whose own full-blown experiment began in the 1930s.[13] Neither England nor Sweden ventured into government-imposed pension programs until the first and second decades of the twentieth century, respectively. The distinction of being the first modern welfare state is usually accorded to Germany, which in the late nineteenth century adopted a series of social-insurance programs that received worldwide notice.

Who was responsible for this achievement? "The welfare state was born in the Germany of Count Otto von Bismarck," writes John Kenneth Galbraith, a champion of welfarism.[14] Bismarck was the master politician who united the states of Germany under the leadership of Prussia in 1871. His social-welfare programs, based on precedents in seventeenth-century and eighteenth-century Prussia, were models for Great Britain, the United States, and the rest of the Western world. Yet he is probably not the figure that welfare-state enthusiasts would have chosen as their guiding light. The quintessential ruthless, repressive, manipulative, and unprincipled politician, Bismarck, the imperial chancellor, excelled at politics — playing domestic and foreign rivals off against each other, forming temporary and shifting alliances of convenience in order to advance his grand agenda for Germany.

A close look at Bismarck's philosophy and achievements will help us to understand the dangers of welfare statism.

A British admirer and contemporary of Bismarck, W. H. Dawson, described him as "the first German statesman who has really tried during the last sixty or seventy years to improve the lot of the labouring population.... He has declared in words that burn, that it is the duty of the State to give heed, above all, to the welfare of its weaker members."[15] According to Dawson, state socialism, the term sometimes used to describe Bismarck's system, was a pragmatic school of thought that rejected the idea that there were fixed economic principles. Economic policy was a matter of expediency determined at a particular time and place. What was good policy in one instance might be bad in another.[16] (This was the position of the German Historical School, which the pioneers of the Austrian school of economics battled.) Dawson described state socialism as being between the extremes of individualism and (revolutionary, internationalist) socialism. Whereas socialism promised to eliminate the prevailing social order, writes Dawson, "State Socialism would use the State for the accomplishment of great economic and social purposes...."[17] It can be called nationalistic, or conservative, socialism.

State socialism's proponents declared it to be a system for ensuring that morality governs economy. Dawson cites Adolf Wagner (1835–1917), a chief German theorist of state socialism, who said, "The relationship of man to man should again be asserted in the economic relationships between persons."[18] Gustav Schmoller, a leader of the German Historical School, said that state socialism seeks "the re-establishment of a friendly relationship between social classes, the removal or modification of injustice, a nearer approach to the principle of distributive justice, with the introduction of a social legislation which promotes progress and guarantees the moral and material elevation of the lower and middle classes."[19]

These theorists emphasized that the group takes precedence over the individual. Self-interest, or what was (and is) sneeringly called "selfishness," must not be permitted to be the central purpose of the social system. Since that is what laissez faire would permit and since the consequences would be unjust, they argued, the state must intervene. Throughout the economic and philosophical literature attacking laissez faire, a distaste for self-interest predominates. It is arguably the major reason why full laissez faire has never been achieved.

Although the state socialists opposed the Marxian call for revolution, they agreed with Marx on many points of economics.[20] Labor, they argued, was at a disadvantage with regard to capital. Wagner held that it was un-Christian to think of labor as a commodity with a market price. Transferring wealth from rich to poor was a proper state activity, he said. He favored state insurance for sickness, accident, and old age, as well as nationalization of some industries; progressive income taxes; and taxes on wealth, inheritances, luxuries, and capital gains. Wagner would have the state expropriate some land and property, such as forests, large farms, and communications and transportation facilities, but that was not a matter of immutable principle because there were no such social and economic principles. If an enterprise was left in private hands, however, it was no less obligated to serve the public weal rather than the personal interests of its nominal owner.

Ludwig von Mises noted two differences between socialism and state socialism. First, whereas socialism (though not the Marxian variety) promised an equal distribution of income (or something close to it), state socialism "makes the basis of distribution the merit and rank of the individual."[21] Individual merit, however, depends on class. Tradition determines the social hierarchy and the rewards for the respective classes. At the top are the monarchy and the nobility, followed by the big landowners, the clergy, professional soldiers, and so on. Peasants, small tradesmen, and laborers all rank ahead of capitalists. Mises remarked, "To the etatist [statist] the worst feature of the capitalist system is that it does not assign income according to his valuation of merit. That a milk dealer or a manufacturer of trouser buttons should draw a larger income than the sprig of a noble family, than a privy councillor or a lieutenant, strikes him as intolerable. In order to remedy this state of affairs the capitalistic system must be replaced by the etatistic."[22]

In other words, the market economy, according to the state socialists, left rewards to the caprice of consumers rather than to the national intelligence bound up in tradition. That must not be permitted.

The second difference between socialism and state socialism, Mises wrote, is that the latter assumes that most people will work not directly for the state but on small farms and in small businesses. The Marxists anticipated large state farms and industrial concerns.[23]

Mises emphasized the conservative nature of state socialism. Its proponents wished to halt innovation and the upsetting of tradition. As Mises put it, "If Marxian Socialism is the social idea of those who expect nothing except through a radical subversion of the existing order by bloody revolutions, State Socialism is the ideal of those who call in the police at the slightest sign of trouble."[24] It's an apt description of a system headed by Bismarck.

The policies of the imperial chancellor, who as prime minister of Prussia in 1862 had declared that the great questions of the day were to be solved not by speeches but by "blood and iron,"[25] were a reaction to a period of German liberalism and free trade that began in the early nineteenth century. Bismarck's program of the 1880s harked back to Prussia's *Landrecht* of 1794, a civil and criminal law code that included a welfare/workfare program for the indigent.[26] As Bismarck said when embarking on his program beginning in 1879: "I do not think that doctrines like those of *'laissez faire,'* ... 'He who is not strong enough to stand must be knocked down and trodden to the ground,' ... should be applied in the State, and especially in a monarchically, paternally governed State."[27] His opponents, he said, left themselves open to the suspicion that they favored the oppression of the rest of society. In succeeding years he pushed for protectionism to preserve German markets for German industry and a series of social-insurance programs to create a safety net for the German workers.[28] Bismarck did not deny that his program overlapped with the socialists' plans: "As soon as a positive proposal came from the Socialists for fashioning the future in a sensible way, in order that the lot of the working-man might be improved, I would not at any rate refuse to examine it favorably," he said.[29]

While trying to assure the owners of capital that he was not their enemy, he emphasized that the state should look out for labor because of its vulnerability. "Give the working-man the right to work as long as he is healthy; assure him care when he is sick; assure him maintenance when he is old," Bismarck said in 1884.[30] When his liberal opponents accused him of proposing socialistic measures, he replied: "Many measures which we have adopted to the great blessing of the country are Socialistic, and the State will have to accustom itself to a little more Socialism yet.... Socialistic is our entire poor relief, compulsory school attendance, compulsory construction of roads...; but if you believe that you can frighten any one or call up spectres with the word 'Socialism,' you take a standpoint which I abandoned long ago, and the abandonment of which is absolutely necessary for our entire imperial legislation."[31]

While Bismarck favored some state monopolies (railways and tobacco, for example), import restrictions, and social insurance, he did not support regulation of factories. He understood that such regulation would be detrimental to firms and their workers. But he did call in 1890 for an international conference on labor issues. "It is the duty of the State so to regulate the duration and nature of labour as to insure the health, morality, and economic wants of the working-men, and to preserve their claim to legal equality," he said.[32]

Social insurance was Bismarck's lasting contribution to the development of the welfare state, in Dawson's words, the "high-water mark of German State Socialism."[33] It consisted of compulsory sickness insurance in 1883, accident insurance in 1884, and old-age insurance in 1889. The last was unprecedented in Germany and Prussia. In 1881, Bismarck's government declared that "the State should interest itself to a greater degree than hitherto in those members who need assistance." This, the government said, was a "duty of humanity and Christianity" and a matter of State preservation.

The State must "cultivate the conception ... that [it] is not merely a necessary but a beneficent institution," and the nonpropertied classes "must, by the evident and direct advantages which are secured to them by legislative measures, be led to regard the State not as an institution contrived for the protection of the better-classes of society, but as one serving their own needs and interests."[34]

This "social element," the government added, is merely "the further development of the modern State idea, the result of Christian ethics, according to which the State should discharge, besides the defensive duty of protecting existing rights, the positive duty of promoting the welfare of all its members, and especially those who are weak and in need of help, by means of judicious institutions and the employment of those resources of the community which are at its disposal."[35] Bismarck at one point made a promise to "remove the legitimate causes of socialism."[36] He also acknowledged the connection between state-provided benefits and compulsion.

When he proposed sickness insurance, Bismarck decided the state should not provide it directly; rather it would be administered through state-created trade organizations. But a year later, his bill for accident insurance called for state provision. "If that is Communism," he said, "I have no objection to it; though with such catchwords we really get no further."[37] Participation was compulsory. For sickness insurance, employers made a nominal contribution. As noted in chapter 2, any employer contribution is really an indirect employee contribution because it is part of the cost of hiring a worker. The deceptive "employer contribution" remains a clever device for maintaining a consensus for the welfare state and for tethering citizens to the government by foreclosing financial independence.

For accident insurance, the employers nominally paid the entire cost. Old-age insurance was for the working class only, with contributions from both employees and employers (again nominal). Benefits could be collected beginning at age 70 (obviously past the average life span) or five years after suffering permanent incapacity.[38] Benefits were also given to widows and orphans.

Bismarck had a larger agenda than merely protecting workers or infusing his government with Christian ethics. He lived at a time when the monarchies were threatened both by classical liberalism and revolutionary socialism. In Germany, the liberals controlled the press, making them a particular source of anxiety for Bismarck. However sincerely he may have wanted the state to take care of workers, he also clearly believed that a conservative, or counterrevolutionary, socialism would stave off the dual threat.[39] In 1884, as Bismarck was in the midst of enacting his social-insurance program, he said, "If the State will show a little Christian solicitude for the working-man, then I believe that the gentlemen of the Wyden [social democratic] programme will sound their bird-call in vain, and that the thronging to them will cease as soon as working-men see that the Government and the legislative bodies are earnestly concerned for their welfare."[40]

The welfare state was not the only method for keeping the social democrats at bay. In 1878, Bismarck also pushed legislative measures to strip them of civil liberties: the Social Democratic Party was outlawed (individuals could, however, run for and hold office); freedom of press, speech, and assembly was eliminated; alleged agitators could be expelled from their homes; gun ownership was restricted.[41] These laws were approved every few years and ended in 1890 when Bismarck was dismissed from office. The founder of the modern welfare state was obviously no friend of liberty.

Other conservatives in Germany supported social insurance to steal the socialists' thunder even before Bismarck. The emperor, William I, saw the program as "affording protection against social-democratic movements."[42] The historian A. J. P. Taylor, referring to this strategy, wrote: "Liberty and Security, the two basic Rights of Man, are no doubt conflicting principles; and refusal of the one has often implied compensation in the other."[43]

Neither the repressive measures nor the welfare state program accomplished their objective. The Social Democratic party did not go away; in fact it continued growing, perhaps because Bismarck would not support factory legislation. That may be why Bismarck lost interest in his social program by 1889.[44] Nevertheless, as a result of the program, the German people were firmly tethered to the state. They developed a stake in its continued growth and their own increasing entanglement. Proposals to reduce the size of government would have been regarded as an attack on their own security when they were sick, injured, and old. Taylor commented, "In a more profound sense it [the program] was successful; it made the German workers value security more than liberty and look to the state rather than to their own resources for any improvement in their condition.... The workers seemed to have received social security as the price of political subservience, and they drew the moral that greater subservience would earn a yet greater reward."[45]

The historian William Harvey Maehl commented, "Whether or not Bismarck's social insurance laws were merely a political stratagem, it is impossible to deny the significance of legislation that for the first time anywhere in history established a state-controlled insurance program against major calamities that beset the poor.... Bismarck demonstrated that a semiauthoritarian monarchy could pioneer social legislation of prime significance.... Bismarck was the pacemaker of the Western world.... Bismarck's ameliorative legislation encouraged nationalist and reformist attitudes among the masses that *insured their loyalty to the state* in World War I."[46]

Another historian, Hermann Beck, has written on the authoritarian Prussian roots of the German imperial welfare state. Prussia was the home of modern bureaucracy and civil service, Beck wrote. "Authority and benevolence," he added, "are the terms that capture best the Prussian state's attitude toward its subjects." Bismarck's social legislation "blazed the trail for the modern welfare state" and typified the bureaucratic assertion that the state could make the people secure.[47]

The inculcation of nationalism and loyalty in Germany cannot help but remind us that, however authoritarian Bismarck was, he was nothing compared to a later German regime. But was there a connection between state socialism and national socialism, or Nazism? Before turning to that question, let us look at the relationship between Bismarck and laissez-faire liberalism.

It would be hard to overemphasize how anti-individualist (antiliberal) the reigning political philosophy of Bismarck's Prussia became. When Bismarck was prime minister of Prussia, a school of conservative social thought known as the "social kingdom" was espoused by Josef Maria von Radowitz, who served as foreign minister, and Bismarck's social policy advisor, Hermann Wagener. These men promoted the view that the working class could be used to stifle the liberal bourgeoisie by tethering workers to the "social monarchy" through measures to improve their material condition.[48] It was the classic political quid pro quo: the state supported the working class's political and economic demands in return for its loyalty against the liberals, who supported such subversive ideas as limited government and free markets. These conservative thinkers "exerted a powerful influence on nineteenth-century Germany. They evinced strong social concerns, far exceeding those of contemporary liberals, and they endowed later welfare legislation with its pronounced patriarchical slant."[49] As the liberal period in Germany faded after the Napoleonic wars and public revenues became tight, the government sought to keep the proletariat from causing trouble, turning to regulation and piecemeal social-welfare measures. It enacted child labor restrictions and poor laws to register rural paupers. Those laws became "formative for Germany's strict system of citizen registration in the twentieth century."[50] (The liberals experienced a resurgence in the 1860s and early 1870s before fading in influence once again.)

Many conservatives idealized the Middle Ages and opposed modernity, including even the centralized monarchy. They hoped to restore the paternalistic decentralized guild system of old. They were especially hostile to liberalism, constitutionalism, the French Revolution, and the Enlightenment. Commerce was anathema. "Where money tinkles, heavenly bells can't be heard," said the publication *Berliner Politisches Wochenblatt*.[51] These conservatives favored an aristocratic order, colonialism, and welfare state institutions in the spirit of noblesse oblige. This group of thinkers, while influential on later conservatives, disappeared from the scene after 1841.

Radowitz was something of a maverick, but still an influential conservative. He favored a constitutional monarchy, but he also believed the state was responsible for solving the problem of poverty. Property rights were too restrictive, he said. He preferred "the inveterate principle that all possessions are but borrowed, each proprietor but a steward of his property, for the use of which he shall be held accountable not only toward the eternal judge but also toward his fellow humans."[52]

The problem of poverty would be solved, Radowitz said, through the "social kingdom." The monarchy would work to improve the workers' lot and in return they would support the regime against the liberal bourgeoisie. Thus for Radowitz, the liberals were more of a threat to the monarchy than the workers. He despised commerce and the market's ranking of money ahead of social standing.[53]

Another Prussian thinker who contributed to modern welfare state thought was Carl Rodbertus. Unlike Radowitz, he was not hostile to industry, but he supported a state-directed manufacturing system to limit "the despotism of profit-yielding possession."[54]

Wagener touted the idea that the loyalty of the lower classes could be won if the state provided for them materially. He expressed his admiration for the ethical idealism of Marx and Ferdinand Lassalle, founder (in 1863) of the first socialist party in Germany; to him that idealism was preferable to the liberals' alleged materialism. Wagener was a communitarian and collectivist who favored state economic planning. He despised liberalism for destroying tradition and communities, setting individuals adrift. He also rejected the "Goddess reason." Attacking industrialists for causing social misery, he called for state control of private enterprise.[55] He later thought that Bismarck's program was too weak.

Bismarck had a direct connection with Lassalle through steady correspondence. Indeed, Lassalle may have strongly influenced him.[56] In 1864, Lassalle wrote to Bismarck expressing his hope that "our common enemy" — the liberals — would be smashed. He also advised that "the working class ... will be prepared, despite its republican convictions ... to accept the crown as the natural champion of a social dictatorship." As a result of this contact, Marx denounced Lassalle for collaborating with Bismarck.[57] Lassalle, F. A. Hayek wrote, was not only a "father" of socialism but also one of "the most important ancestors of National Socialism."[58]

As for the relationship between the Prussian conservative welfare statists and Nazism, Beck and Hayek see a definite link. The state ideology of the social conservatives, writes Beck, "helped make Hitler, who frequently invoked it, acceptable to those Prussians to whom otherwise he might have been too common and uncouth." Some of the conservatives' ideas "proved a powerful lever to rally conservative Germans behind Hitler." Those ideas helped bring socialism and conservatism together. "And ironically enough," Beck adds, "the only 'social kingdom' Germany history knew was the Third Reich."[59]

Beck writes that the Nazis were interested in and drew open parallels with the Prussian social legislation of the 1850s and 1860s. This included poor relief and registration and surveillance of paupers to prevent abuse of the system.[60] The historian Adalbert Hahn wrote that the conservatives and their ideas "signified the first emergence of national socialist ideas in German politics." Adolf Richter wrote during the Nazi years in reference to Wagener: "Comparisons with the present become perfectly obvious." Walter Früh, looking to Radowitz, wrote that national socialism is "suited to a rekindling of interest in the ideas of German social conservatives in the age of early capitalism."[61] But in guarding against overstating the case, Beck notes that the Nazis had an obvious interest in claiming that their policies merely continued earlier German traditions. Nevertheless, the similarities between the two sets of economic policies cannot be denied. Beck calls the Prussian conservatives "precursors of the radical conservatism of the twentieth century and even fascism."[62]

Hayek writes, "'Conservative Socialism' (and, in other circles, 'Religious Socialism') was the slogan under which a large number of writers prepared the atmosphere in which 'National Socialism' succeeded."[63]

Avraham Barkai acknowledges "the process of rapprochement between the Nazis' economic principles and those of other groups in the rightist camp that took place toward the end of the Weimar Republic. This rapprochement was a result of contemporary realities, but it also grew out of the common ideological and spiritual soil that nourished the rightist revolution."[64]

We may witness the similarities between the economic ideas of Prussian conservatism and Nazism by consulting the views of an undisputed authority, Adolf Hitler. Hitler spent no little time expounding his economic views. In 1931, two years before taking power, he wrote (after insisting that his party supports property):

> What matters is to emphasize the fundamental idea in my party's economic program clearly — the idea of authority. I want the authority; I want everyone to keep the property he has acquired for himself according to the principle: benefit to the community precedes benefit to the individual. But the state should retain supervision and *each property owner should consider himself appointed by the state*. It is his duty not to use his property against the interests of others among his own people. This is the crucial matter. The Third Reich will always retain its right to control the owners of property.[65]

Barkai quotes several Nazis who attributed their economic ideas to German conservatives. Although he would not say that Nazism was the only possible outcome of the tradition or that the earlier theorists were Nazis, "Nevertheless, one should not belittle the influence that this tradition exerted on economic reality in the twenties and thirties.... In Germany large and influential groups were mentally prepared to accept and absorb the same ideas because it was possible to refer them to a continuum of tradition.... An influential section of university economists, senior government officials, and businessmen in Germany had been brought up and educated in a tradition that made them more receptive to these new theories than their peers in other countries."[66]

Gustav Stolper went further: "Without the preliminary work done by their predecessors, Hitler and National Socialism would not have been possible.... Hitler had only to press a button for the previously prepared mechanism to start operating. His predecessors had already done whatever was necessary for him. The inclination toward state economy, alive in German history since the establishment of the Reich under Prussia's leadership, had now reached its climax."[67]

The system wrought by Bismarck and bequeathed to his political heirs throughout the West obviously had monumental consequences. Henry Gaullieur observed the political and economic developments in Germany (and the rest of Europe) during Bismarck's time and commented: "The continental nations created the only monopoly against which there never is any redress at all — except revolution and armed resistance — the monopoly of the paternal state.... The life of a new citizen or subject does not really belong to him, but to the State, for by another legal statute he is taught that he should be ready at all times to sacrifice his life, not for his own interests or those of his family, but for the political ambition of his government." Referring to state-run education, he noted, "The State has 'Mind Overseers' ... and they alone determine whether a man is useful or worthless."[68]

Gaullieur saw the effects of welfare statism on average people. "In all such measures leading originally to the founding of a paternal state," he wrote, "what was intended by the people to be a safeguard became only a stumbling block; what was meant to be a philanthropic stimulant changed to a stupefying drug, a paralyzing weight; what might have acted as a shield in the hands of guardian angels became a poisoned weapon in the hands of bureaucrats, impelled by ordinary human instincts and passions. As a matter of course, the worse the machine worked, the more it had to be enlarged and strengthened, and the more it grew."[69]

Specifically in Germany, wrote Gaullieur, the public education system, which is at the center of every welfare state, aimed only to create functionaries. "Its object is not to make a man," he wrote, "but an officer, a soldier, a German mandarin, or a politically worthless subject."[70]

Writing from the United States during the Progressive Era, the European-born Gaullieur saw the threat from paternalism to his adopted country. He warned that oppressive government could start modestly and grow out of the almost menial actions of average men. "The State must in the end always turn out to be practically a number of more or less intelligent human beings sitting in public buildings — generally on upholstered chairs — surrounded by a vast crowd of their own delegates, all working for wages, generally from nine or ten o'clock to sundown, all liable, like other men, to be wise or foolish, honest or dishonest, conscientious or not.... If the doctrine of paternalism of the State is once recognized as the panacea for all political ills," he wrote, "it depends only upon accidental circumstances whether the tutelary protection, to be extended over the land to secure the much-coveted national welfare, shall end in mild despotism or in a reign of terror."[71]

The most prominent critic of the collectivism that was beginning to sweep the West was the English liberal philosopher Herbert Spencer. Indeed, he was the symbol of laissez faire and the target of every collectivist. A despairing Spencer said in 1885 that he would no longer write about politics: "The wave of opinion carrying us toward socialism and utter subordination of the individual is becoming irresistible."[72] In his classic work, *The Man Versus the State*, he described and analyzed what he called "The New Toryism" and "The Coming Slavery."[73]

The New Tories were classical liberals, Spencer wrote, who confused rectifying evil, which was the liberal legacy, with achieving good. The mixed-up liberals now thought that the mission was to use coercive methods to bring about good directly, rather than leaving people free to achieve their own good. "Most of those who now pass as Liberals, are Tories of a new type," he wrote.[74]

In his essay "The Coming Slavery," Spencer wrote, "All socialism involves slavery."[75] How so?

> The essential question is — How much is [a person] compelled to labour for other benefit than his own, and how much can he labour for his own benefit? The degree of his slavery varies according to the ratio between that which he is forced to yield up and that which he is allowed to retain; and it matters not whether his master is a single person or a society. If, without option, he has to labour for the society, and receives from the general stock such portion as the society awards him, he becomes a slave to the society. Socialistic arrangements necessitate an enslavement of this kind; and towards such an enslavement many recent measures, and still more the measures advocated, are carrying us.[76]

Of course, Gaullieur and Spencer were not heeded. Germany was to become a model for the United States and England. To the rising intellectual class, Germany represented the latest stage in the natural evolution of the state. As we'll see in the next chapter, American intellectuals would flock there to observe and to study and to bring back political blueprints that would be followed throughout most of the twentieth century.

Notes

[1] See Bruce L. Benson, "Where Does Law Come From?" *The Freeman: Ideas on Liberty,* December 1997, pp. 725–33.

[2] Hernando de Soto describes mercantilism in detail in *The Other Path: The Invisible Revolution in the Third World* (New York: Harper & Row, 1989), chapter 7, "The Parallel with Mercantilism."

[3] Gertrude Himmelfarb, *The Idea of Poverty: England in the Early Industrial Age* (New York: Alfred A. Knopf, 1983), p. 4.

[4] Ibid.

[5] Ibid., pp. 252–56.

[6] Ibid., p. 211.

[7] It should be pointed out that many Fabians, such as the prominent Sidney and Beatrice Webb, were also enthusiastic about imperialism and eugenics. That was no accident. These are forms of the social engineering, or "rational planning." See Gertrude Himmelfarb, *Poverty and Compassion: The Moral Imagination of the Late Victorians* (New York: Alfred A. Knopf, 1991), pp. 364–68. In this connection, note that the Associated Press reported on August, 25, 1997, that the model Swedish welfare state sterilized 60,000 citizens, adults and children, between 1935 and 1976. According to the AP, "They were found to be 'inferior,' flawed by bad eyesight, mental retardation or 'undesirable' racial characteristics." The AP added, "Not only did eugenics foresee an improved human race, it also was appealing to Social Democrats, who were beginning to see that Sweden's welfare state would be costly and wanted to limit the number of people who would have to be supported, the newspaper [the prestigious *Dagens Nyheter*] said." The program was supported by welfare state architect Gunnar Myrdal. See Dan Balz, "Sweden Sterilized Thousands of 'Useless' Citizens for Decades," *Washington Post,* August 29, 1997, p. A1. Presumably, the Swedish officials agreed with George Bernard Shaw, the playwright and Fabian, who said, "We must eliminate the Yahoo or his vote will wreck the commonwealth." Himmelfarb, *Poverty and Compassion*, p. 368.

[8] Jack D. Douglas, *The Myth of the Welfare State* (New Brunswick, N.J.: Transaction Publishers, 1989), p. 183.

[9] Quoted in Himmelfarb, *Poverty and Compassion,* p. 311.

[10] Himmelfarb, *Poverty and Compassion,* p. 311.

[11] Ibid.

[12] Ibid. p. 382. My thanks to historian Ralph Raico for putting

this quotation in context. More on Bismarckism below.

[13] Sweden's dramatic economic growth, which began in the nineteenth century, preceded its plunge into welfare statism. See Peter Stein, "Sweden: From Capitalist Success to Welfare-State Sclerosis," Policy Analysis no. 160, September 10, 1991, Cato Institute, Washington, D.C.

[14] John Kenneth Galbraith, *Economics in Perspective: A Critical History* (Boston: Houghton Mifflin Co., 1987), p. 210.

[15] W. H. Dawson, *Bismarck and State Socialism: An Exposition of the Social and Economic Legislation of Germany since 1870* (London: Swan Sonnenschein & Co., 1890), p. ix.

[16] The United States has intellectuals in this tradition. John Dewey said, "The person who holds the doctrine of 'individualism' or 'collectivism' has his program determined for him in advance. It is not with him a matter of finding out the particular thing which needs to be done and the best way, under the circumstances, of doing it. It is an affair of applying a hard and fast doctrine which follows logically from his preconception of the nature of ultimate causes." Quoted in George Dykhuizen, *The Life and Mind of John Dewey* (Carbondale, Ill.: Southern Illinois University Press, 1973), p. 228. Odd, isn't it, that people who say things like that never seem to support laissez faire under *any* circumstances.

[17] Dawson, p. 2.

[18] Quoted in ibid., p. 3.

[19] Quoted in ibid.

[20] As Ludwig von Mises points out, the Marxian prediction of the withering away of the state is not what distinguishes socialism from state socialism, since the state cannot actually disappear under any form of socialism. See Ludwig von Mises, *Socialism: An Economic and Sociological Analysis,* trans. J. Kahane (London: Jonathan Cape, 1936), p. 245.

[21] Mises, p. 245.

[22] Ibid., p. 246.

[23] Ibid., pp. 247–48.

[24] Ibid., pp. 248–49.

[25] John A. Garraty and Peter Gay, eds., *The Columbia History of the World* (New York: Harper & Row, 1972), p. 911.

[26] Dawson, p. 19.

[27] Quoted in ibid., p. 29.

[28] The historian Erich Eyck writes, "German protectionism furthered and strengthened German nationalism.... It is no mere chance that the nationalist and anti-Semitic movements in the German universities began after the victory of protectionism and Bismarck's break with Liberalism." Erich Eyck, *Bismarck and the German Empire* (New York: W.W. Norton, 1968), p. 259.

[29] Quoted in Dawson, p. 45.

[30] Quoted in ibid., pp. 34–35.

[31] Quoted in ibid., pp. 63–64.

[32] Quoted in ibid., p. 106.

[33] Ibid. p. 109.

[34] Quoted in ibid., p. 111.

[35] Quoted in ibid.

[36] Quoted in ibid., p. 113.

[37] Quoted in ibid., p. 119.

[38] It should be noted that in the industrial world, life expectancy would not hit 65 until about 1950. In the late nineteenth century, life expectancy was about 45.

[39] Bismarck did not mention his social-insurance program in his memoirs, which indicates the intensity of his interest in the matter. Gordon A. Craig, *Germany: 1866–1945* (New York: Oxford University Press, 1978), p. 150.

[40] Quoted in Dawson, p. 35.

[41] A. J. P. Taylor, *The Court of German History: A Survey of the Development of Germany since 1815* (New York: Capricorn Books, 1962), p. 119, p. 130, and Craig, p. 96.

[42] Dawson, p. 111.

[43] Taylor, p. 130. Taylor errs in regarding "security" provided by someone else as a right. Rights do not conflict. If one must apparently give up some liberty — to the state — to achieve security, one's security is actually undermined. See also Edward Crankshaw, *Bismarck* (New York: Viking Press, 1981), p. 378.

[44] Hajo Holborn, *A History of Modern Germany: 1849–1945* (Princeton, N.J.: Princeton University Press, 1969), p. 292.

[45] Taylor, p. 130.

[46] William Harvey Maehl, *Germany in Western Civilization* (University, Ala.: University of Alabama Press, 1979), pp. 476–78; emphasis added. Maehl says the classical liberals in Germany kept the

social-insurance program from being more comprehensive.

[47] Hermann Beck, *The Origins of the Authoritarian Welfare State in Prussia* (Ann Arbor, Mich.: University of Michigan Press, 1995), p. viii.

[48] Beck, p. ix.

[49] Ibid.

[50] Ibid., p. x.

[51] Quoted in ibid., p. 57.

[52] Quoted in ibid., p. 68.

[53] Ibid., pp. 70–75.

[54] Ibid., pp. 93–99.

[55] Ibid., pp. 112–13. Beck writes that Wagener influenced the development of the Nazi movement but adds that it would be an overstatement to call him an intellectual precursor of that movement.

[56] Garraty and Gay, p. 891.

[57] Beck, pp. 110–11.

[58] F. A. Hayek, *The Road to Serfdom* (Chicago: University of Chicago Press, 1944), p. 168.

[59] Beck, p. 122.

[60] Ibid., pp. 156, 165.

[61] The quotations are in ibid., pp. 234, 239.

[62] Ibid., p. 259.

[63] Hayek, p. 180.

[64] Avraham Barkai, *Nazi Economics: Ideology, Theory, and Policy,* trans. Ruth Hadass-Vashitz (Oxford: Berg Publishers Ltd., 1990), p. 27.

[65] Quoted in ibid., pp. 26–27. Emphasis is mine.

[66] Ibid., p. 102.

[67] Quoted in ibid., p. 105.

[68] Henry Gaullieur, *The Paternal State in France and Germany* (New York: Harper & Brothers, 1898), pp. xi, 7–9.

[69] Ibid., p. 10.

[70] Ibid., p. 168.

[71] Ibid., pp. xi–xii.

[72] Quoted in Himmelfarb, *Poverty and Compassion,* p. 310.

[73] Herbert Spencer, *The Man Versus the State* (1884; Indianapolis: LibertyClassics, 1981). The essays in the book can also be found in *Herbert Spencer: Political Writings,* ed. John Offer (Cambridge, Mass.: Cambridge University Press, 1994).

[74] Spencer, p. 5.

[75] Ibid., p. 55.

[76] Ibid., pp. 56–57.

4

The Idea of the Welfare
State in America

Ideas have consequences. Richard Weaver's immortal book title has become a cliché, which is a tribute to its power and truth. The development of the welfare state in the United States dramatically illustrates the power of ideas, in this case, wrong ideas.

The American people did not start out with welfare state ideas. On the contrary, the consensus appears to have been oriented to what is today disparagingly called "rugged individualism."[1] That term sums up an attitude that essentially holds that people ought to look after their own lives and not expect government to take care of them. This outlook has nothing to do with so-called atomistic individualism, which would hold the hermit up as the model human being. Early American rugged individualism meant instead voluntary action in the service of self, family, and voluntary local community. Americans were certainly not against banding together by choice to achieve things they couldn't achieve individually. Alexis de Tocqueville observed the proliferation of associations during his travels in the young United States: "Americans of all ages, all stations in life, and all types of dispositions are forever forming associations. There are not only commercial and industrial associations in which all take part, but others of a thousand types — religious, moral, serious, futile, very general and very limited, immensely large and very minute."[2] Such voluntary joining together was apparently unprecedented in human history and unknown elsewhere at the time. It sounds like something people would do when they don't

65

expect government to do for them.

This is not to say that all Americans held a perfectly consistent philosophy about the liberty and limits of government. Of course they didn't. Nor did the Founders and political leaders of the day. From the beginning, there were advocates of (relatively) big government. The competing economic and political philosophies espoused by Alexander Hamilton and Thomas Jefferson capture the political drama of the age. Hamilton wanted, and got, a (relatively) strong central state. Jefferson was a decentralist who wanted a weak national government. Hamilton wanted, and got, a national bank. Jefferson opposed it. Hamilton stood for what we today call industrial policy, or corporate welfare. Jefferson took the more libertarian line of little or no government interference in economic matters. Hamilton wanted a protectionist trade policy. Jefferson favored free trade.[3]

The late historian Jonathan R. T. Hughes documents a surprising amount of government authority to intervene in the economy going back to colonial times. Hughes wrote that "the tradition of law from England gave government even at the lowest levels extensive power to establish, disestablish, and regulate economic activity of all kinds. As far as colonial America was concerned, there never was an absence of such controls, a time of complete economic freedom."[4]

But that should not blind us to the unprecedented degree of economic freedom that existed in the early days of the United States. Power was not always exercised, and laws on the books were not always enforced. People could go about their business with little interference from government — certainly by today's standards. Government at all levels spent little — perhaps 5.5 percent of "national income." The federal government alone today spends more than 20 percent. "Most Americans paid no taxes whatsoever to federal officials directly," writes the historian Jeffrey Rogers Hummel, "and their only regular contact with any representatives of central authority was probably through the United States Post Office — if they had any contact all."[5]

But something happened. A country that began with a strong libertarian consensus turned statist somewhere along the way. How a society goes from libertarian to statist is obviously a complex story, with countless factors and currents. In America, the story involves nationalists, socialists, populists, Progressives, social democrats, Marxists, Fabians, and more. The interplay among thinkers of various stripes and the corresponding popular movements is something no one can hope to understand perfectly. This chapter will attempt to identify some important intellectual developments that account for the transition.

While early America always had its advocates of activist government, that view becomes more prominent after the Civil War. Economic conditions can of course spawn "reform" movements. The problems for farmers after the Civil War helped launch the populist movement, an essentially agrarian crusade for government regulation of the economy and ownership of railroads and other "public utilities." Agitation for government activism also emerged in reaction to the visible pockets of wealth that developed in the early days of industrial capitalism. Even though much of that wealth resulted from the pioneering, productive efforts of entrepreneurs, which benefited the bulk of citizens, there were envious people who thought such fortunes perforce had to be ill-gotten. Of course, some wealth at that time, as now, was obtained through political favoritism, including subsidies and tariffs. But anti-capitalists rarely distinguished the two ways of amassing wealth: production and exploitation.

From Europe, socialism tried to establish itself as the dominant radical movement in the United States. Its Marxist variation did not have large appeal, leaving most socialists no choice but to move in a "conservative direction."[6] In 1901, the Socialist Party under Eugene V. Debs called for social insurance and government ownership of trusts, but, as Arthur A. Ekirch Jr. writes, it "reflected the increasingly moderate, nonrevolutionary position of those radicals and reformers who, in each country, espoused what was variously called a social democratic, prolabor, or progressive political stance."[7] These and other movements can be seen as tributaries feeding into a larger political movement, Progressivism and then later the Democratic Party, although the socialists maintained an independent party for some time. Progressivism was an interventionist program with a heavy nationalist orientation. As Eldon Eisenach puts it, "Progressives were nationalists to the core."[8] That bothered socialist radicals who suspected compromise and moderation. But Progressivism established itself as a contending political doctrine and lives on today in both "right" and "left" variants. (Whether a Progressive is on the "right" or "left" depends on whether his emphasis is on corporate welfare or labor-underclass welfare.)

The Civil War itself and its militaristic effect on American society had important consequences for the nationalist collectivization of America that occurred in the following decades: it encouraged collectivist intellectuals to vigorously promote their reform visions, and it won thinkers to the collectivist cause. It even convinced some individualists that the world had changed, making their world-view outdated.

The war's military collectivization of society profoundly impressed some Northern intellectuals, giving them visions of a new world. The war effort devalued the individualism that had characterized the earlier Jeffersonian America. Service to the Union became the reigning ideal. Order, explicit planning, and regimentation rose in value. Independent thought seemed more a liability than an asset.

The war, wrote the historian Allan Nevins, "transformed an inchoate nation, individualistic in temper and wedded to improvisation, into a shaped and disciplined nation, increasingly aware of the importance of plan and control."[9]

A symbol of that change in mindset is Ralph Waldo Emerson, the transcendentalist author of *Self-Reliance,* who before the war represented a distinctively American cantankerous individualism opposed to institutions and their impositions on the person.[10] When the war came along, Emerson expressed approval that it imposed obligations on everyone. He hoped no one would be exempt from "the public duty." In a 180-degree turn, he assigned government and civilization priority over "the private man." In "American Civilization," written in 1862, he was willing to grant government "the absolute powers of a dictator" in a crisis. "Emerson's characteristic emphasis on individualism and anarchism disappeared."[11]

In Emerson's words, "War organizes [and] forces individuals and states to combine and act with *larger* views."[12] Self-reliance was now replaced by service and obedience, particularly in the military. His new views influenced his outlook on culture, as evidenced by his support for a state-created National Academy of Literature and Art. A new era required new thinking.

After the war, intellectuals were more interested in a strong central government and nationalism. Jeffersonian decentralization and individual liberty were seen as part of the old ways, made obsolete in the new postwar America. The Declaration of Independence became old-fashioned. What Eisenach says about the Progressives applies to the postwar intellectuals: their views were in "direct opposition to an abstract rights-based discourse, whether expressed as individual rights, as States' rights, or as constitutional formalism."[13]

Unlike poetry before the war, poetry now rhapsodized on the glory of the nation. Herman Melville wrote about empire, not freedom.[14] The crushing of the Southern secession demonstrated the need for strong government and citizen compliance with the state.

As a result, there was increasing tolerance of tyranny in Russia and France. Frederickson comments, "The Civil War, by making the very concept of 'revolution' or 'rebellion' anathema to many Northerners, had widened the gulf that separated nineteenth-century Americans from their revolutionary heritage."[15] The conservative Orestes Brownson stated that the mission of America "is not so much the realization of liberty as the realization of the true idea of the state."[16] Wendell Phillips, a leader of the libertarian abolitionist movement before the war, ran for governor of Massachusetts after the war on a welfarist platform.

The new thinking about American society could be found among religious conservatives and secular "radicals." The point is not that all those intellectuals were explicit advocates of the welfare state. Rather, their efforts to replace individualism with nationalism and reverence for strong government couldn't help but give encouragement to anyone who wished to use government to provide services and transfer wealth. Jeffersonian decentralization was an impediment to the service/transfer state. Anything that weakened the earlier ethic and resulting institutional barriers was a boon to welfarism.

It is in the postwar period that the social sciences began their rise to prominence. The objective of those new disciplines was not knowledge for its own sake. "They [the new social scientists] sought the 'laws' underlying social, economic, or legal phenomena in the hope of finding ways to discipline society and control its events."[17] Those intellectuals also saw themselves as most suited to wield influence if not power itself in the new, rationally planned society. Eisenach calculates that of the nineteen most prominent authors of "Progressive public doctrine," nine were founding members of the American Economic Association; nine others helped start the American Sociological Association.[18]

The collectivist intellectuals believed that the Civil War held important lessons for the new America. It wasn't war itself that they valued, but the things that war brought. John W. Draper, for example, wrote that war taught subordination and stimulated an appreciation of order. Men, said Draper, "love to obey" those they believe are their intellectual superiors. "In military life they learn to practice that obedience openly," he said, adding that individualism was to blame for the war.[19]

What intellectuals such as Francis A. Walker, Charles Francis

Adams Jr., and future U.S. Supreme Court Justice Oliver Wendell Holmes Jr. wished for was, in Frederickson's words, a "continuance ... of the crisis mentality of war." That mentality would maintain the sense of duty to society that was palpable during the war. While those men wanted conservative objectives served, others, such as John Wesley Powell, had "humanitarian" ends in mind.[20]

The problem for these thinkers was that peacetime did not inspire service and sacrifice. People became centered on their own lives, their families, and immediate communities. But war was a call to duty and the "strenuous life." If only a substitute for war could be found, a call to duty that did not involve bloodshed. "There is one thing I do not doubt," said Holmes, "and that is that the faith is true and adorable which leads a soldier to throw away his life in obedience to a blindly accepted duty, in a cause which he little understands, in a plan of campaign of which he has no notion, under tactics of which he does not see the use."[21]

The philosopher William James also wished for a "moral equivalent of war," a way to marshal the spirit of selfless service under government direction without the unpleasantness of combat. He advocated conscription of young people for civilian service in mines, road building, and fishing boats "to get the childishness knocked out of them." Praising the "martial virtues," James called for the "surrender of private interest" in favor of "obedience to command."[22]

This theme — that individual liberty, private property, and laissez faire were "selfish" — recurs throughout the collectivist and Progressive literature. Thus, if selfishness was bad, then its institutions were thereby condemned. This fit nicely with the religious views of many of the reformers. Baptist theologian and reformer Samuel Zane Batten wrote in *The Christian State,* "Just so far as democracy means the enthronement of self-interest and the apotheosis of individual desire ... so far it becomes an iniquitous and dangerous thing." He also said, "True liberty means the voluntary sacrifice of self for the common life."[23] Another clergyman-activist, George Herron, was blunter: "Sin is pure individualism."[24]

It was during the Civil War that an incipient national social-welfare agency was established. The United States Sanitary Commission was a semi-official relief organization recognized by President Lincoln. Run by the elite of society, it was intended not only to render war relief but also to reorient society toward service and discipline after the war. Key to the thinking of the commission's leadership was that policymaking should be in the hands of the elite. Its leader, Henry W. Bellows, saw in the war "God's method of bringing order out of chaos."[25] (Bellows, a conservative, believed in the divine right of kings. "The head of state *is* a sacred person. It is not the policy but the *strength* of the government that is to save us."[26])

After the war, the first bona fide welfare program was started at the national level. This was the pension system for Union veterans. A program with such an apparently narrow purpose would not seem a promising way to launch the welfare state, but it was useful in demonstrating the political payoff in tethering citizens to the state. In her book *Protecting Soldiers and Mothers,* Theda Skocpol wrote that by 1889, thanks to the expanding Civil War pension system, "the United States had become a precocious social spending state."[27] More than a third of elderly Northern men and a good many other men, along with widows and dependents, drew quarterly checks from the U.S. Pension Bureau that year. The benefits could be more generous than those offered by European welfare states.[28] Between 1880 and 1910, pensions made up a quarter of the national budget. In 1910, 28 percent of all American men, more than 42 million, got an average $189 a year. More than 300,000 widows, orphans, and other dependents received money too.[29]

What's important about the system is that the Republican Party quickly learned that the pension system could be used to buy votes, a form of institutionalized bribery. A Civil War pension system should shrink, as veterans die. Strangely, it did not shrink, but grew. After seeming to peak after 1870, the system began expanding again, peaking in the 1890s. The commissioner of pensions in 1891 boasted that the pension bureau was "the largest executive bureau in the world," with a staff of 2,000 and a brand new headquarters.[30]

Why? Because the Republican-controlled government systematically liberalized eligibility to win political favor. Congressmen could even propose bills to grant pensions to individuals, and they did so often as favors. By 1910, nearly 1,000 such bills were sponsored each session.[31] "Accordingly, after the mid 1870s, the number of pensioners and the costs resumed upward trajectories and continued to grow until the facts of generational mortality overtook the ingenuity of politicians at channeling ever higher benefits to ever more people."[32] Skocpol points out that the Arrears Act of 1879 turned a disabilities program into a patronage program.[33] Promising and delivering benefits was an effective way to get reelected. Democrats such as Grover Cleveland hit the program for its extravagance and fraud. The Republicans devoutly defended it and profited from it.

The pension system as model for the welfare state can be overdrawn. Unlike Bismarck's pension program, the American system was not automatically available to all citizens. And ironically, the Progressives, as "good government" advocates, were repelled by its corrupt patronage, making many of them reluctant to advocate a generalized government pension system before other political reforms were erected.[34] That attitude was expressed by Harvard University president Charles Eliot in 1889, when he said that "one cannot tell whether a pensioner of the United States ... is a disabled soldier or sailor or a perjured pauper who has foisted himself upon the public treasury."[35] Even so fervent a fan of Bismarck's pension plan as John Graham Brooks said, "I do not see how we can save any pension system in this country from running to politics."[36] Charles Francis Adams condemned the Civil War pension program for its "legislative incompetence" and "political corruption."[37]

Yet even if collectivist individuals feared corruption in the short run, they held dear their war-inspired vision of a future of solidarity freed from rampant individualism and competition. No one better exemplifies the profound influence of the Civil War on the intellectuals than Edward Bellamy, author of the highly influential novel *Looking Backward*. As a child during the war, Bellamy became preoccupied with military discipline. It deeply affected him and shaped his thinking as an adult. In 1889 he wrote a short story, "An Echo of Antietam," in which he described a group of men marching to join the Union army. "The imposing mass," Bellamy wrote, "gives the impression of a single organism. One forgets to look for the individuals in it, forgets that there are individuals." He lamented that the martial spirit could not be preserved without the hostility of war. "What a pity that the tonic air of battlefields ... cannot be gathered up and preserved as a precious elixir to reinvigorate the atmosphere in times of peace, when men grow faint of heart and cowardly, and quake at the thought of death."[38]

Bellamy took this so seriously that he drew up a blueprint — presented in the form of a novel — for a new society built along military lines but without warfare as the objective. Even though Bellamy and his intellectual allies eschewed the horrors of war, they could not help but concede its value. Bellamy's protagonist, Dr. Leete, states that "occasional wars ... were absolutely necessary to prevent your society, otherwise so utterly sordid and selfish in its ideas, from dissolving into absolute putrescence."[39]

Looking Backward: 2000–1887 was published in 1888. It sold 60,000 copies the first year and more than 100,000 the next, including European sales. It eventually sold a million copies. The book made Bellamy a hero and the leader of a movement that he called "Nationalist." (He felt socialism and Marxism were divisive along class lines and therefore harmful.) Followers of Bellamy, mostly in the middle class, set up 150 Nationalist Clubs and a publication, *Nationalist Monthly Magazine*. This movement, writes historian Ekirch, "helped to make socialist doctrines and ideas respectable in the United States."[40] It did that, in part, by "introducing a non-Marxist, noninternationalist outlook into the process of Americanizing socialism."[41]

Bellamy's book also influenced a host of avowed collectivist intellectuals in the coming years. Among those whose thinking was shaped by Bellamy were John Dewey, Upton Sinclair, Clarence Darrow, and Roger Baldwin. A large group of lesser known intellectuals and activists were also changed by Bellamy's book.[42]

In *Looking Backward* they found a model for a new society. That model was based on "the ethics of solidarity derived in large part from its author's mystical interpretation of the Civil War."[43] What began as a fable, Bellamy later wrote, evolved into "the vehicle of a definite scheme of industrial organization."[44]

Bellamy's vision was sweeping if it was anything. The plot revolves around Julian West, who falls asleep in 1887 and awakens in the year 2000 to find that America has been transformed into a society dedicated to the "material and moral welfare of the whole body of the sovereign people to the highest point ... that is to say, an equal level."[45] It is an egalitarian, collectivist America. For Bellamy, economic equality was merely the counterpart of the political equality that motivated the American Revolution, although the Founders were not aware of the connection.

Bellamy's thesis is at the center of the intellectual change that occurred in the late nineteenth and early twentieth century. In this period, the label "liberalism" went from meaning limited government and essential laissez faire to meaning activist government and economic interventionism. It is sometimes suggested that the transformation of the term "liberal" was a strategic move by statists to appropriate a benign label from their enemies. That may have been true. But it seems that the appropriation was also the result of a misunderstanding. The political revolutions of the eighteenth century, especially the American Revolution, were partly based on the ideals of self-government and political equality — the democratic spirit if not literal majoritarian democracy.

It is plausible that some liberals could have erroneously applied those principles to economic affairs. If the people should vote to choose political leaders, they reasoned, why shouldn't they also decide economic matters that affect them as much as political matters do? Just as those intellectuals feared the concentration of political power, they also feared the concentration of economic "power." They were willing to accept political power as a counterweight. The philosopher John Dewey spoke for many of his fellow intellectuals when he said that "persons acutely aware of the dangers of regimentation when it is imposed by government remain oblivious of the millions of persons whose behavior is regimented by an economic system through whose intervention alone they obtain a livelihood."[46] The collectivists' mistake was in not realizing that economic "power," the ability to produce what people want to buy, is nothing like political power, the ability to legally force people to act against their will. The collectivists could not tell the difference between firing someone and firing *at* someone.

It should also be pointed out that collectivist opponents of laissez faire were divided into those who wanted to break up the large corporations for a return to the world of small enterprise (the populists), and those who saw the value of large enterprises but wanted to harness them in the "public interest." The former group favored vigorous prosecution of the trusts, while the latter, such as Theodore Roosevelt, distinguished "good trusts" from "bad trusts." Eisenach points out that the Progressives disliked "small-producer capitalism" with its competition and consequent moral defects. They preferred big (regulated) organizations, including big unions, without competition.[47]

Bellamy was in the latter category. He clearly mistook economic "power" for political power and built his novel on that error. But he approved of bigness as long as it was properly controlled and devoted to society's interests. He believed that breaking up concentrations of capital would bring only an equality of poverty. But capital must not be left in the hands of selfish private interests. Rather, it should be held by "a single syndicate representing the people, to be conducted in the common interest for common profit." As a result, the new America into which Julian West awakens is organized as one big corporation. The nation "became the one capitalist in the place of all other capitalists; the sole employer, the final monopoly in which all previous and lesser monopolies were swallowed up, a monopoly in the profits and economies of which all citizens shared. The epoch of trusts had ended in The Great Trust."[48]

In Bellamy's vision, everyone works for the nation and everyone is paid the same. There is no competition. People are motivated by patriotism, duty, and service. They understand, says Dr. Leete, that it is "their duty to contribute their share to the economy." When the nation became the only employer, "citizens, by virtue of their citizenship, became employees, to be distributed to the needs of industry." The idea of service is so natural, Dr. Leete says, that no one regards it as compulsory.[49] But it *is* compulsory. There is no other way to make a living except through the state firm. Someone who tried to escape the system "would have ... committed suicide."[50] An able person who refuses to do his duty "is sentenced to solitary imprisonment on bread and water till he consents."[51]

Bellamy likened his plan to universal military service and referred to the work force as an "industrial army." While his system tries to match people to the jobs they wish and are suited for, the ultimate decision belongs to the government. Work is compulsory from age 21 to 45, with all workers spending the first three years at manual labor. Everyone is paid the same nominal salary, in the form of a credit card representing an equal share of the national product. But not all incomes are really the same. When Julian West asks Dr. Leete what happens when one job has a surplus of workers and another a shortage, the doctor replies that the length of the work day is adjusted to equilibrate the number of jobs and the number workers. Of course, that means that those who work fewer hours are paid more per hour than those who work more hours, a point that Bellamy does not address. Also, the most meritorious are awarded special privileges, again compromising Bellamy's quest for equality.

Yet, according to the author, all are entitled to an equal share of the national product, regardless of ability. All people, says Dr. Leete, are "co-inheritors of the human race's achievements that make production possible. To not give them a share is to rob them."[52]

Bellamy's new world is filled with restrictions. No "capricious changes" in employment are permitted. There is no money. The credit card may be used only at official stores. (There are no private stores.) There is no way to transfer credit from one person to another, so private buying and selling cannot take place.[53] "Buying and selling," explains Dr. Leete, "is considered absolutely inconsistent with the mutual benevolence and disinterestedness which should prevail between citizens and the sense of community which supports our social system. According to our ideas, buying and selling is essentially anti-social in all its tendencies."[54]

Each citizen gets his full year's credit on the first of the year. For extraordinary expenses, heavily discounted advances from the next year's credit can be obtained. A "reckless spendthrift" would have his spending controlled by the authorities.

Credit cannot be accumulated year to year, except for special anticipated needs. In other words, savings is prohibited and seen as a vice. Why? "No man has any more care for the morrow, either for himself or his children, for the nation guarantees the nurture, education, and comfortable maintenance of every citizen from the cradle to the grave."[55]

The virtue of this new society for Bellamy is that competition is banished because all needs are taken care of. That implies, of course, that the law of scarcity is repealed. Bellamy says as much, but insists throughout his book that human nature has not changed. Here the author leaves some rather important issues unaddressed. Scarcity is a feature of our world because people's wants are unlimited and resources at any given time are not. The necessity for tradeoffs is ubiquitous. In Bellamy's world, the social system would limit how much people want. Dr. Leete explains that people would not accumulate goods beyond a narrow range of need because the cost of storing the goods would be prohibitive and the private sale of surplus goods could not take place. (As noted, he assumes, wrongly, that people would not barter.) He adds that people accumulate so little that there is no need to prohibit or tax inheritances.

With insecurity and competition eliminated, people behave differently from how they behaved in the nineteenth century, Dr. Leete explains. For example, store clerks don't care whether shoppers buy or not. They can't lose their jobs if sales fall. So not only do they abstain from promoting products, they are actually ignorant about the goods they handle.

The national administration determines what will be produced and how much. Prices are set according to the labor it takes to produce the goods. Bellamy provides no detail on how this is to work. He wrote his book before the Austrian economist Ludwig von Mises, beginning in 1920, showed that without private ownership of producer's goods — and the trade and *market prices* private ownership generates — no economic calculation, and therefore no intelligent planning, can be accomplished. If disparate inputs, including raw materials, machines, land, and labor services, cannot be stated in a common monetary unit, then alternative production plans cannot be compared in order to ascertain which is the most economical. No way will exist to determine whether the value to consumers of a given finished product is higher or lower than anything else that could be produced with the same inputs. Presumably, Bellamy would want the optimal output (in the consumers' estimation) for a given supply of resources, but his system would preclude that.

Moreover, as Mises's student, F. A. Hayek, wrote, information relevant to production is scattered throughout society, often in tacit form, and not held by any single mind or small group. Critical information is thus forever inaccessible to central planners. That fact makes Bellamy's aspiration impossible.[56]

The key fallacy in central planning is to treat a collection of interacting individuals — society — as a single living entity with one mind and one value scale. That fallacy is exhibited in the words of Simon Patten: "The final victory of man's machinery over nature's control of human society was the transition from anarchic and puny individualism to the group action as a powerful, intelligent organism."[57]

While central planning was often justified as the application of reason and intelligence to the economy as a whole, it is in fact something quite different: the suppression of intelligence at the individual level (including coordination of individuals in the market) and the substitution of pseudo-intelligence. For reasons already mentioned, the virtue in an individual's planning of his own projects and enterprises cannot be turned into an argument for economy-wide planning.

Thus, despite his glowing vision, Bellamy's world would be characterized by economic chaos. Among his inadequacies is his failure to understand how competition and entrepreneurship uncover the ignorance and error that keep resources from best satisfying consumers. For Bellamy, competition and entrepreneurship are wasteful and should be banned. "Competition," his protagonist says, "which is the instinct of selfishness, is another word for dissipation of energy, while combination is the secret of efficient production."[58] In a world of omniscient human beings, Bellamy might have a point about wasteful competition. But not in our world of ignorance where we don't know what we don't know. It is through competition, as Ludwig von Mises, F. A. Hayek, Israel Kirzner, and other Austrian economists have taught, that we learn things we would not have learned otherwise. The world holds the possibility of surprise — the discovery of unimagined opportunities to improve people's lives. The potential for entrepreneurial profit encourages alertness to those opportunities. Banning profit and entrepreneurship precludes that discovery and thus makes people worse off than they would have been.[59]

Bellamy also missed another point: competition and cooperation are not at odds. They are complementary features of a laissez-faire economy and of individual liberty itself. This should be too obvious to need special attention. What are the market, division of labor, and specialization, if not cooperation on a grand scale? If people are free, it follows that they are free to choose with whom they will cooperate. Where there is such choice in means of cooperation, there is competition. Two shoe sellers seeking customers are competing to cooperate. To regard that as wasteful is to assume that all knowledge about satisfying people's shoe needs has already been discovered and that there is nothing left to learn. But of course that is not true. There is always more to learn, particularly because consumer preferences change.

Two other points about Bellamy are noteworthy. He and his colleagues believed they were not just setting forth an attractive vision but were predicting the future according to the principles of social evolution. His school of thought was as "Darwinist" as any laissez-faire advocate's, including the collectivists' archenemies, Herbert Spencer and William Graham Sumner. In this view, Jeffersonian notions of liberty and decentralized power might have been appropriate to an earlier stage of social evolution, but not to the present stage. By so arguing, Progressives could "scientifically" dispense with individual rights and constitutional limits on government power.[60] Indeed the Constitution was no more than something to be got around. Herbert Croly, a leading Progressive, denounced the "monarchy of the Constitution."[61] This was a position the Progressives bequeathed to their New Deal descendants.

Bellamy also portrayed his collectivist system as liberating for the individual. He and other collectivists believed that the way to free the person was to take personal economic decision-making out of his hands. Unburdened by the necessity of making a living, each person would be truly free to reach his potential. To put it another way, they believed that real freedom requires the abolition of choice and self-responsibility: individualism through collectivism. That is in sharp contrast with the classical liberal, or libertarian tradition, which holds, as Charles Murray writes, that it is self-responsibility that makes life important rather than trivial.[62] Could life in the industrial army, with all choices made by the authorities, seriously be construed as liberating?

Bellamy's philosophy demonstrates a fundamental claim of the present book. His "humanitarian" intention was to relieve each person of responsibility for his own existence. Material security would be guaranteed. Want would be abolished. But the price of security would be the individual's right to make important decisions about his own life, that is, his humanity. Despite the liberation language, citizens would be tethered to government, and the leash would be short indeed. Control would be pervasive. Everyone would be an employee and tenant of the state, subject to its caprice and potential for brutality. Even if the government could deliver on its promise of material welfare — which it could not — that loss in liberty would never be acceptable to clear-thinking, rational human beings. Liberty is too important, too central to man's humanity, to be given up even for material security. After all, the exercise of reason, our basic means of survival, requires the freedom to act on our individual judgment. Reason and liberty go together.

Although Bellamy rejected the title "socialist," because of its class-conflict connotations, revolutionary means, and internationalism, he nonetheless accepted the socialist program of collective ownership of the means of production. Other reform writers, although they might have preferred full socialism, were willing to settle for less — pervasive regulation and government ownership of selected industries — out of a sense of pragmatism and political realism. Even so, Bellamy had a strong influence on those thinkers. He gave life to the collectivist program.

Bellamy had ample allies. Another Darwinist, Lester F. Ward, also proposed cooperation and rational planning in place of competition and laissez faire. "The individual has reigned long enough," Ward stated. "The day has come for society to take its affairs into its own hands and shape its own destinies."[63] Other writers in this vein included Charles H. Cooley and Edward A. Ross. Their Reform Darwinism provided an intellectual underpinning for the Progressives' political movement.

The self-styled "collectivists" Bellamy influenced were also enamored with Germany, which, as we've seen, was the first modern welfare state, thanks to the policies of Chancellor Otto von Bismarck. Before 1914 (when Germany became a pariah because of the Great War), American students who would go on to become influential intellectuals did their graduate work in the social sciences at German universities, where the Ph.D. was inaugurated. Eisenach notes that twelve of the nineteen prominent Progressive writers studied in Germany, four of them earning doctorates there.[64] These included Richard T. Ely, later a founder of the American Economic Association and a leading advocate of government intervention. American students "returned fired with a new sense of the social uses of history, sociology, and economics."[65] In particular, their training instilled an appreciation for the state and its power to create social reform. Hegelianism, for example, held that the state embodied the highest ideal and the divine spirit.

Ely and his colleagues strove to familiarize America with European social democracy. He did not embrace full-blown socialism but he had a rather expansive and paternalistic view of the state. "The state, and state alone, stands for all of us," Ely said.[66]

The German-educated American intellectuals saw themselves as specially anointed, by virtue of their training, to "work out the generalized schemes for regulating [the] new society."[67] They claimed to have the insight and knowledge to override individual choice, which was seen as a obsolete notion. Like Bellamy, they wished to organize society along the lines of an industrial organization, that is, the corporation they so admired but misunderstood. Here they neglected a basic distinction often pointed out by F. A. Hayek. A corporation is specifically organized to achieve a declared end, the production of a particular product in order to make money. The people who choose to join that organization share that end. Society, in contrast, does not share a single end or even a single hierarchy of ends. Rather, its members each have their own scale of values. Liberty, property, the rule of law, and the other pillars of Western liberalism (libertarianism) permit people to pursue different ends in peace and cooperation. A modern prosperous society does not require agreement on objectives and preferences. It requires agreement only on means, namely, a commitment to peaceful interaction and a rejection of violence. The collectivists' wish to transform society into a grand organization would necessitate the imposition of ends on individuals who would undoubtedly believe they have other things to do with their time and resources.[68]

Oblivious to the distinction between an organization (or corporation) and society, the Progressives saw the industrial trust as the model for the future society. The Twentieth Century Fund wrote, "The perfect form of the trust is the state."[69] The spokesmen for organizing society as a trust were elitist and had little confidence in the ability of people to make decisions for themselves. "It is obvious," said Maurice Parmelee, "that the average citizen is not and can never be competent to perform many of the governmental functions, especially the more important of these."[70] Accordingly, thinkers such as Parmelee disliked democracy and favored government by expert commissions.[71]

This contempt for the people showed up in their views regarding public opinion also. As Eisenach puts it, public opinion was to be turned into "an engine of social control."[72] Echoing Rousseau's theory of the general will, the Progressives believed that public opinion wasn't merely what a collection of individuals thought and wanted. That was selfish interest. Public opinion was something elevated and collective. And if the people didn't see it that way, then the elites would take matters into their own hands, molding opinion according to what wise rulers understood to be necessary. As Edward Ross wrote in his book *Social Control,* "The contents of the social mind are superior to the contents of the ordinary individual mind."[73]

This sort of thinking helped launch the Progressive Era, which saw the creation, beginning in 1887, of national agencies of economic regulation: the Interstate Commerce Commission, Food and Drug Administration, Federal Trade Commission, Federal Reserve System.[74] It was also the period for legislation such as the Sherman Antitrust and Clayton acts, which ostensibly combated monopoly, and the income tax.[75] Despite popular impression, important businessmen were often in sympathy with the Progressive program, which could be made to coincide with their immediate economic interest. For example, some businessmen saw national regulation both as a way to "rationalize" unpredictable markets (and safeguard profits) and to preempt more radical policymakers in the states, who had been winning regulatory victories.[76] This was consistent with the thinking of Progressives who preferred large regulated economic organizations to "cutthroat competition." Historian Robert Higgs writes, "Yet what was most significant about their [the businessmen's] position was the belief that greater governmental intervention was inevitable.... That Bigger Government had come to be seen as irresistible ... signaled a profound transformation of the ideological environment."[77] Perhaps they were not immune to the Progressives' cultural indoctrination. Their not infrequent statements about wealth's being a public trust had a definite Progressive flavor.

When the United States entered the European war in 1917, it provided further opportunity for the intellectuals to put collectivist ideas into practice. (The Progressive movement largely shed any pacifist sentiment it had expressed previously and supported the war.) As Higgs writes, "More than anything the Progressives had achieved, war undercut American liberties and fed the growth of Big Government."[78] The War Industries Board and other agencies brought the whole economy firmly under the guiding hand of government. Progressivism yielded war socialism. That experience whetted the appetite of many intellectuals and businessmen for a more permanent form of government intervention, sometimes called industrial democracy.[79]

The connection between war and Progressivism was not strained. Woodrow Wilson was elected president on a Progressive platform, then led the United States into the war in order to remake the world.[80] War and international intervention can be seen as counterparts to domestic intervention. Reprising the thinking that occurred during the Civil War, many Progressives, John Dewey among them, saw in war the opportunity for a grand national purpose. (It was while Progressives were beating the drums for war that dissident Randolph Bourne wrote, "War is the health of the State."[81])

Herbert Croly, a founder and editor of *The New Republic,* justified U.S. entry into the war on the grounds that the nation needed "the tonic of a serious moral adventure." He feared for the future of the United States if the individual could forgo national service and simply concentrate on his own life.[82] Here is the mark of the Progressive, or collectivist, mind. Private concerns were petty and unworthy. National crusades were grand and ennobling.

Croly published an influential book in 1909, *The Promise of American Life,* in which he chided his Progressive allies for being too individualistic. He embraced the muscular central government of Hamilton, and rejected Jeffersonianism. Calling his philosophy "the New Nationalism," Croly endorsed government control of corporations in order to achieve an equitable distribution of wealth. He also favored a strong military policy so that America could bring enlightened policies to the rest of the world.

He summed up his outlook thus: "The Promise of American Life is to be fulfilled not merely by a maximum amount of economic freedom, but by a certain measure of discipline; not merely by the abundant satisfaction of individual desires, but by a large measure of individual subordination and self-denial."[83]

Croly, like many of his colleagues, saw his philosophy as a middle way between laissez faire and Marxism. His influence rivaled Bellamy's. Among those whose thinking was shaped by him were Theodore Roosevelt, who used Croly's "New Nationalism" ideas in his second, unsuccessful run for the presidency in 1912; Felix Frankfurter, who would become a U.S. Supreme Court justice; Henry L. Stimson, the future secretary of state and secretary of war; and journalist Walter Lippmann.

Most important, Croly's thinking helped shape the world-view of the architects of the New Deal under Franklin Roosevelt. It was the New Deal that so firmly clamped the welfare state, at the national level, on the United States. Among other things, it included a national pension program (Social Security) and comprehensive regulation of banking and labor relations, and set the precedent for further intervention in subsequent decades. As the twentieth century drew to a close, the nation had still not seen a serious effort to dismantle the Roosevelt edifice, despite the ideological pronouncements of White House occupants.[84]

It is possible to make too much of the New Deal, to treat it as a radical break with the past. It was not such a radical break.[85] It was more of what had gone before, but it was much more. In its first phase, it attempted a cartelization of business and agriculture. When the U.S. Supreme Court blocked those measures, it slightly changed course, enacting regulation of business and labor, establishing a federal welfare program, and imposing a Social Security scheme modeled on Bismarck's social-insurance program. (The Supreme Court began giving President Roosevelt majorities after he attempted to "pack" the Court.)

William E. Leuchtenburg, an eminent historian of the New Deal, has written that Roosevelt and his advisors had familiarized themselves with a massive amount of political thinking. They were influenced by the populists, urban social reformers, and "John Dewey's conviction that organized social intelligence could shape society."[86]

Yet most influential, according to Leuchtenburg, were the New Nationalists, including Herbert Croly. "Roosevelt's advisers of the early New Deal scoffed at the nineteenth-century faith in natural law and free competition; argued for a frank acceptance of the large corporation; and dismissed the New Freedom's [that is, Woodrow Wilson's] emphasis on trust-busting as a reactionary dogma that would prevent an organic approach to directing the economy."[87] The top members of the Brain Trust wanted the government to cooperate with business, but they differed on how much influence business would be permitted to have.

Rexford Guy Tugwell was one of the most prominent collectivist voices in the Roosevelt administration. In writings before FDR was elected, Tugwell promoted interventionist ideas. In a 1925 textbook, he took what he characterized as the middle ground between laissez faire and socialism and embraced a system "in which free competition can be combined with centralized control in infinite degrees and methods." As he and his coauthors elaborated, "A regime which is basically capitalistic may advantageously forget at times the old dogma of the inviolability of private property, as well as its vain hope of completely free competition." Of course, it is government that decides when to let "blind struggles take their course" and when to consciously guide the economy.[88]

Tugwell complained that in the marketplace, luck determines incomes as much as ability. He believed that most people could be persuaded that "every one [sic] should have at least a minimum subsistence" provided by government. He also favored government aid to people who were not poor. He sensed a weakening of respect for private property when it conflicts with "desirable ends," such as equal opportunity and support for the arts and sciences.[89]

Not all of the Brain Trusters were as "left wing" as Tugwell. But despite differences among Roosevelt's advisors, however, they put a permanent stamp on the twentieth century. The degree of government power in the coming years would be adjusted at the margins. But it would not be substantially reduced. The welfare state seemed to be here to stay.

The ideology of activist government, whether it was called the welfare state, the New Nationalism, industrial democracy, or state socialism, had many sources from the American farm to American intellectuals with German Ph.D.s to the European socialists and British Fabians. War, unsurprisingly, played a significant role in stimulating collectivist thinking, not only because government always grows in war, but because the apparent social unity and subordination of individuals gave collectivist intellectuals something to strive for.[90] Bellamy, Croly, and others made the most of their opportunities and promoted their vision of the organic state directed from the center and acting as a single organism with a single set of objectives. They did much to create an atmosphere in which the laissez-faire ideas of Adam Smith and Thomas Jefferson were seen as out of date and in need of replacement by the interventionist ideas of Alexander Hamilton, Otto von Bismarck, and the European socialists.

Notes

[1] See Joseph R. Stromberg, "Tensions in Early American Thought," *The Freeman: Ideas on Liberty,* May 1999, pp. 44–50.

[2] Alexis de Tocqueville, *Democracy in America,* trans. George Lawrence, ed. J. P. Mayer (1848; New York: Perennial Library/Harper & Row, 1988), p. 513.

[3] Arthur A. Ekirch Jr., *The Decline of American Liberalism* (New York: Atheneum, 1976), pp. 37–72.

[4] Jonathan R. T. Hughes, *The Governmental Habit: Economic Controls from Colonial Times to the Present* (New York: Basic Books, 1977), p. 8.

[5] Jeffrey Rogers Hummel, *Emancipating Slaves, Enslaving Free Men: A History of the American Civil War* (Chicago: Open Court, 1996), p. 222.

[6] Arthur A. Ekirch Jr., *Progressivism in America: A Study of the Era from Theodore Roosevelt to Woodrow Wilson* (New York: New Viewpoints, 1974), p. 41.

[7] Ibid., p. 44.

[8] Eldon J. Eisenach, *The Lost Promise of Progressivism* (Lawrence, Kansas: University Press of Kansas, 1994), p. 5.

[9] Quoted in George M. Frederickson, *The Inner Civil War: Northern Intellectuals and the Crisis of the Union* (New York: Harper Torchbooks, 1968), p. 111.

[10] Ibid., p. 180. This account of Emerson's change of heart is drawn from Frederickson's book.

[11] Ibid., p. 177.

[12] Quoted in ibid.; emphasis added. In collectivism, the individual and his concerns are always small.

[13] Eisenach, p. 5.

[14] Frederickson, pp. 184–85.

[15] Ibid., p. 187.

[16] Quoted in ibid.

[17] Ibid., p. 202.

[18] Eisenach, pp. 31–36. The American Economic Association's 1885 proposed platform states: "We regard the state as an educational and ethical agency whose positive aid is an indispensable condition of human progress. While we recognize the necessity of individual initiative in industrial life, we hold that the doctrine of laissez faire is unsafe in politics and unsound in morals; and that it

suggests an inadequate explanation of the relations between the state and the citizens." (Ibid., p. 138.)

[19] Frederickson, pp. 200–201.

[20] Ibid., pp. 215–16.

[21] Quoted in ibid., p. 220.

[22] Quoted in ibid., pp. 235–36.

[23] Quoted in Eisenach, pp. 187, 189.

[24] Quoted in ibid., p. 188.

[25] Quoted in Frederickson, p. 111; see also pp. 98 and 109.

[26] Quoted in ibid., p. 136; emphasis in original.

[27] Theda Skocpol, *Protecting Soldiers and Mothers* (Cambridge, Mass.: Belknap Press of Harvard University Press, 1992), pp. 1–2.

[28] Ibid.

[29] Ibid., p. 65.

[30] Ibid., pp. 107ff., 120.

[31] Eisenach, p. 153.

[32] Skocpol, p. 110.

[33] Ibid., p. 120.

[34] Ibid., p. 2.

[35] Quoted in ibid., p. 267.

[36] Quoted in ibid., p. 271.

[37] Ibid., p. 275.

[38] Quoted in Frederickson, p. 226.

[39] Quoted in ibid., p. 228. Imagine war being seen as a cure for selfishness!

[40] Ekirch, *Progressivism in America*, pp. 41–42.

[41] Ibid., p. 42.

[42] John L. Thomas, "Introduction," p. 85, in Edward Bellamy, *Looking Backward: 2000–1887,* ed. John L. Thomas (1888; Cambridge, Mass.: Harvard University Press, 1967). Also see James Gilbert, *Designing the Industrial State: The Intellectual Pursuit of Collectivism, 1880–1940* (Chicago, Quadrangle Books, 1972), pp. 16, 22–24.

[43] Thomas, p. 2.

[44] Quoted in ibid.

[45] Bellamy, p. 83.

[46] Quoted in George Dykhuizen, *The Life and Mind of John*

Dewey (Carbondale, Ill.: Southern Illinois University Press, 1973), p. 293.

[47] Eisenach, pp. 145–47.

[48] Bellamy, p. 127.

[49] Ibid., p. 131.

[50] Ibid., p. 132.

[51] Ibid., p. 175.

[52] Ibid., p. 181.

[53] Bellamy, apparently ignorant of how money spontaneously develops, errs here. People could secretly engage in barter with each other. Then through barter, a readily tradable medium of exchange would emerge. At that point, a full black market would develop.

[54] Ibid., p. 148.

[55] Ibid., p. 149.

[56] For more on the impossibility of central planning, see F. A. Hayek, ed., *Collectivist Economic Planning: Critical Studies on the Possibilities of Socialism* (1935; Clifton, N.J.: Augustus M. Kelley, 1975).

[57] Quoted in Gilbert, p. 45.

[58] Bellamy, p. 254.

[59] Most useful here is Israel Kirzner's work on entrepreneurship, including *Competition and Entrepreneurship* (Chicago: University of Chicago Press, 1973).

[60] Eisenach, p. 109.

[61] Quoted in ibid., p. 73.

[62] See Charles Murray, *What It Means to Be a Libertarian: A Personal Interpretation* (New York: Broadway Books, 1997).

[63] Quoted in Ekirch, *Progressivism in America,* p. 23.

[64] Eisenach, pp. 31–36.

[65] Gilbert, p. 74.

[66] Quoted in Ekirch, *Progressivism in America,* p. 27.

[67] Gilbert, p. 16.

[68] See F. A. Hayek, *The Constitution of Liberty* (Chicago: University of Chicago Press, 1960).

[69] Quoted in Gilbert, p. 34.

[70] Quoted in ibid., p. 35.

[71] The choice between rule by majority vote and rule by aloof

experts is a false alternative. The classical liberal, or libertarian, alternative of self-rule in the market order is the only one consistent with liberty and prosperity.

[72] Eisenach, p. 74.

[73] Quoted in Eisenach, p. 76.

[74] At the municipal level, the Progressives favored unelected commissions to perform functions that were previously the responsibility of elected officials.

[75] See Terry Anderson and P. J. Hill, *The Birth of the Transfer Society* (Stanford, Calif.: Hoover Institution, 1980) for a political and legal history of the origins of the modern American welfare state.

[76] See Gabriel Kolko, *The Triumph of Conservatism: A Reinterpretation of American History, 1900–1916* (New York: The Free Press, 1963) and Robert Higgs, *Crisis and Leviathan: Critical Episodes in the Growth of American Government* (New York: Oxford University Press, 1987), pp. 114–15.

[77] Higgs, p. 115.

[78] Ibid., p. 123.

[79] See Murray N. Rothbard, "War Collectivism in World War I," in *A New History of Leviathan: Essays on the Rise of the American Corporate State,* ed. Ronald Radosh and Murray N. Rothbard (New York: E. P. Dutton and Co., 1972), pp. 66–110.

[80] Eisenach writes that the Progressives distrusted Wilson before his election because he defended the states' police power under the Constitution and had a more limited view of federal regulation than they had (Eisenach, p. 125).

[81] Randolph S. Bourne, "The State," in Bourne, *War and the Intellectuals: Collected Essays, 1915–1919,* ed. Carl Resek (New York: Harper Torchbooks, 1964), p. 71.

[82] Ekirch, *Progressivism in America,* p. 266.

[83] Herbert Croly, *The Promise of American Life* (1909; New York: E. P. Dutton and Co., 1963), p. 22.

[84] The one exception was the elimination of Aid to Families with Dependent Children, the national welfare program. See chapter 5.

[85] Those who think the 1920s saw a retrenchment from the Progressive Era should see Randall G. Holcombe, "Federal Government Growth before the New Deal," *The Freeman: Ideas on Liberty,* September 1997, pp. 547–51. On the policies of President Her-

bert Hoover in particular, see Murray N. Rothbard, "Herbert Clark Hoover, A Reconsideration," *New Individualist Review* 4 (Winter 1966): 3–12, and Rothbard, "Herbert Hoover and the Myth of Laissez-Faire," in Radosh and Rothbard, pp. 110–45.

[86] William E. Leuchtenburg, *Franklin D. Roosevelt and the New Deal, 1932–1940* (New York: Harper Torchbooks, 1963), p. 33.

[87] Ibid., p. 34.

[88] Rexford Guy Tugwell, Thomas Munro, and Roy E. Stryker, *American Economic Life and the Means of Its Improvement* (New York: Harcourt, Brace and Co., 1925), p. 444.

[89] Ibid., p. 434.

[90] See Higgs for a pathbreaking history of how war and preparation for war racheted up the power of the state.

5

What About the Poor?

Calls for abolition of the welfare state are bound to be met with the words, "But what about the poor?" Although the welfare state consists of much more than benefits for low-income people, that will tend to be the first question asked. The welfare state is synonymous with help for the poor, although that is a small part of what it does.

People are at least abstractly concerned about people who have low incomes. That doesn't mean people are willing and eager to give up a huge percentage of their own income to help them. But it is surely true that most of us would prefer that there were no people in distress. That is a sign of basic benevolence.

Adam Smith recognized the limits of benevolence in *The Theory of Moral Sentiments*.[1] Our benevolence typically ripples outward in decreasing intensity, forming a pattern like the one generated by a stone tossed in a lake. Or, as Smith's contemporary, David Hume, put it, "A man naturally loves his children better than his nephews, his nephews better than his cousins, his cousins better than strangers, where everything else is equal."[2]

The point is that no one should be expected to be equally concerned about every person on earth or even in the country. Public policy based on that presumption is bound to create problems. Yet first lady Hillary Rodham Clinton was fond of saying, "There is no such thing as other people's children." What that means is that each person should regard each child — in the city, state, country, world? — as his own. Does that sound realistic? Or desirable? Of course not. But from such absurd sentiments (or demagoguery) come palpably inane government programs. If government can instill a little guilt, it can get away with much. We should identify it for what it is: the exploitation of people's benevolence.

Since I wrote a book calling for the abolition of the government schools, I am often asked how the poor will be able to afford education for their children in a privately financed system. People understand that among its other features, so-called public education is a transfer program. Some people pay more in taxes than is spent on their children (if they even have children), and that surplus is spent on the schooling of children whose parents pay less in taxes than it costs. It is a subtle transfer. But call for an end to public schooling and many people will bring up the issue.

In the same way that many think the poor would not be educated unless the government transferred money from higher-income (which doesn't mean "rich") people, they think the poor would lack many other essential goods and services — housing, food, medical care, shoes — without the welfare state. Predictions of starvation in the streets are not unheard of.

The political exploitation of the poverty issue seems to know no bounds. Government is looked on as the benevolent provider of nearly all things. There are those, such as Vice President Al Gore, who thought the government should guarantee low-income people access to the Internet. The Internet, of course, has become increasingly important. But if the government is to guarantee computers and Internet services to everyone, what won't it try to guarantee? Exercise equipment is good for healthful living. Perhaps the government should buy everyone a treadmill or subsidize membership in athletic clubs. And how about the various forms of relaxation that require money? Are those candidates for government subsidy as well? Why should anyone have to go without a VCR and access to video stores?[3]

The point is that once government begins to look after the welfare of people, there is no stopping point. As noted in chapter 2, the dynamics of interest-group politics will exert pressure for government to offer more and more services and to broaden the definition of "needy." (If budget deficits make overt provision by government impractical, subtle ways, such as mandates on employers, will be found.) One politician seeking reelection will propose some new benefit, calculating that it will win him votes. Then to win votes in Congress or the state legislature, he will agree to vote for a colleague's proposal to expand the benefit to others not originally included (again to win voter support) or to vote for a new benefit altogether for the colleague's constituency. This is known as "logrolling," a common practice that impels the growth of government. It is one reason why hopes for a modest welfare state tend to be unrealistic. Programs intended for the poor grow to include the middle class, whose support is needed for passage. Once set in motion, the dispensing of benefits expands, at least until a fiscal crisis stuns the public, forcing cuts, or more commonly, cuts in the rate of growth.

The irony is that even if a welfare state gets started solely to help the poor, the perverse dynamism of pressure-group politics will proliferate programs for the nonpoor, stunting the growth of the economy and harming the very poor who were supposed to be helped by the system.[4]

It is easy to point out systemic flaws in the democratic welfare state. Nevertheless, we still have this question: what of the poor? How will they fare if the welfare state is abolished? This is not as straightforward a matter as it may seem. What does "poor" mean? Surely, it does not mean simply having a low income or low standard of living. There are lots of people with low incomes and living standards whom we do not consider poor. Consider a fresh graduate of Harvard Medical School or Yale Law School. As he goes into the job market, he may have an income of zero. What's more, he may have huge student loans to repay. Looked at purely in material terms, he is poor. But we don't think of him that way. That's because he has something the poor don't seem to have: prospects. That graduate has invested heavily in income-producing knowledge and skills, and so it is only a matter of time before he has a high income and the means to get out of debt. His future, materially speaking, is bright. Hence, we don't think of him as poor.

"Prospects" doesn't mean simply that others recognize the graduate's potential and are willing to give him a chance. The concept sums up volumes about character and virtue, including the graduate's possession of a serious frame of mind, a long time-horizon and the willingness to defer gratification, self-responsibility, self-respect, and self-control. Alas, many people who seem relegated to perpetual poverty lack just those virtues. That lack may have many *reasons* (irresponsible and abusive parents, for example), but no *causes*. In other words, too many individuals have risen above bad conditions and have prospered for us to permit ourselves to think that people's fate is determined by their childhood. Lawrence E. Harrison's book title, *Underdevelopment Is a State of Mind,* refers as much to individuals as it does to nations.[5]

A question worth asking is whether the welfare state can provide people with prospects in the broad sense used here, or whether the logic of the welfare state actually works against its "benefici-aries" in that regard. An indicative statistic on this issue is that poor people who don't get government welfare are two and a half times more likely to leave the ranks of the poor within a year than people on the dole.[6] This speaks volumes. Does welfare dispensed by gov-ernment agencies encourage personal characteristics that undermine independence and other desirable things? Common sense says yes.[7] And that is not contradicted by the fact that a large number of people don't remain on welfare all their lives. If a significant number do remain on welfare long-term, it would have bad effects on them as well as society at large. Even those who leave the dole early may be corrupted by it; the dole delayed their independence and perhaps helped to plant bad habits. If the dole instills ways of living that preclude a person's developing prospects, the system undercuts its stated goal of providing people with the hope for an independent and dignified life. The welfare state is a cruel hoax on those vic-tims.

There is certainly reason to think that welfare has a malign effect on a significant number of recipients. Breaking the relation-ship between work and income, subsidizing out-of-wedlock births, and encouraging the creation of single-parent families can't be good for anyone. (Recent reforms, including work requirements, were a long-belated recognition of these effects.) The message that some-one owes you a living has the power to rot souls. Much harm was done by the "welfare rights" movement of the 1960s in the name of removing the stigma from being on the dole. Being the ward of an impersonal bureaucracy can't do much for one's sense of self-worth. Many people who get a taste of that experience may find it revolting and break free of it to become self-sufficient. But many others will take the path of least resistance and allow themselves to be cor-rupted. They are responsible for that, of course, but the welfare state is an accomplice in dehumanization. As economist Alan Reynolds put it, "The welfare state, in its broadest sense, is not kind but cruel. It has undermined the American dream for those who receive gov-ernment transfer payments and for those who pay the bills."[8]

On the issue of welfare rights, nothing could be more absurd. Rights are principles that create a zone of sovereignty around each individual. The idea that someone can have a right to someone else's wealth subverts the very concept of rights and therefore cannot be valid. The only legitimate rights are the rights to take action with respect to one's own person and to the material objects (property) one produces or acquires through voluntary exchange or gift. The foundation of rights is the value of life and each human being's need for liberty.[9]

The matter of prospects is only the beginning of the difficulty in defining what it means to be poor. Ultimately the definition will be arbitrary. Calculation of a poverty line will reflect countless debatable assumptions. Even the idea of bare subsistence is not clearcut. The U.S. government officially defines poverty in terms of a specific package of food. An income that is less than triple what it takes to buy that package is defined as below the poverty level. The definition is premised on what percentage of income the average American family spent on food around 1955 (about one-third of income).[10] Thus, in 1997 the poverty line for a family of four was $16,400.[11]

The government has offered many other definitions of poverty. Michael Tanner writes that the Census Bureau has about thirty definitions. Depending on which one is used, the percentage of the population in poverty will range from 8.5 to 21.1 percent.[12] The figure used by the Clinton administration is 13.3 percent.[13] The late Henry Hazlitt pointed out that in 1962 the government said the poverty line was $3,000 before taxes. But in the same document, Hazlitt wrote, the government noted that the nation had 5.4 million families with incomes less than $2,000. "How could these 17 million persons exist and survive if they had so much less than enough 'to satisfy minimum needs'?" Hazlitt asked.[14] Subjectivity abounds.

Statistical measures of poverty run up against the problem of relativity. In an important sense, it is uninformative to say that someone is poor if he is, say, in the bottom fifth of the income "distribution."[15] The bottom fifth in the United States is far richer than the bottom fifth in most other places. It's wealthier than the upper fifths in many places. Being poor here is not the same as being poor in Ethiopia or even most of Europe.

Nor is being poor here the same as being poor here in the past. It takes less and less time and effort to acquire more and more comforts, not to mention necessities. As economists W. Michael Cox and Richard Alm write, in terms of the work time required to buy things (the real price) "the cost of living in America keeps getting cheaper.... Free markets have routinely brought the great mass of Americans products once beyond even the reach of kings."[16] Using the "average hourly wage for production and nonsupervisory workers in manufacturing," Cox and Alm calculate the following: Comparing 1919 with 1997, the work time it takes to buy half a gallon of milk dropped from 39 minutes to 7 minutes; a pound of ground beef, 30 minutes to 6 minutes; a dozen oranges, 1 hour and 8 minutes to less than 10 minutes.[17] The examples can be multiplied.

As American society gets richer, some people will always be in the bottom fifth. That's a statistical certainty. Nevertheless, they will be richer than they were before, just as they are richer than at any time in the past. Moreover, it is perfectly consistent for the gap between "rich" and "poor" to be growing even as the poor get richer. Imagine an elevator of which the ceiling and floor both rise although the distance between the two is increasing. Should we still call the people at the bottom poor? By what standard?

This issue has been discussed for centuries. Is poverty absolute or relative? Adam Smith wished to define it in relative terms. The poor lacked "necessaries." "By necessaries," Smith wrote in *The Wealth of Nations,* "I understand, not only the commodities which are indispensably necessary for the support of life, but whatever the custom of the country renders it indecent for creditable people, even of the lowest order, to be without."[18]

Smith's conception of poverty would make it a never-ending problem. That would suit the political leaders, the bureaucrats who run the welfare bureaus, and the lobbyists who make their living off the welfare state. But it would make "keeping up with the Joneses" a basis for public policy. These days consumer goods that didn't even exist a few years ago are commonplace, even for the "poor." When the parents of the baby boomers were young they did not have videotape recorders, computers, wireless telephones, or even central air conditioning. Should we regard as poor anyone who does not have the money for those things even if they can afford adequate diet, clothing, shelter, and other necessities and amenities? By relative standards, the middle class in 1950 was poor compared to many people we call poor today.

Indeed, the poor here are richer than the general population of Western Europe. According to the Census Bureau, in the early 1990s people officially designated "poor" in the United States owned household appliances in greater proportion than the *general populations* of many European countries. For example, 60 percent of the poor here own VCRs. That is larger than the percentage of the general population owning VCRs in Belgium, Denmark, France, Germany, Italy, the Netherlands, Spain, Sweden, and Switzerland. In the United Kingdom, the proportion of people owning VCRs was 65 percent, only slightly above the American "poor." Again, the American poor owned microwave ovens and clothes dryers in greater proportion than many European nations. While only 20 percent of

American poor owned dishwashers, that compared favorably with the United Kingdom, where only 11 percent had that household convenience. The Census Bureau reports that 93 percent of the poor have color televisions.[19]

This says something about how we measure poverty. Statistics show that for people in the lowest fifth of incomes, household consumption is actually double reported income. That can result from unreported jobs, family support, or savings.[20] That so many welfare recipients work on the sly says something about the entrepreneurship of people who are classified poor and about what they would do if welfare were abolished.[21]

The preoccupation with income categories is the subject of much fallacious thinking. Moral judgments about the gap between the bottom and top fifths is misleading, especially when it fails to take account of education (people with more education tend to make more money than people with less education), age (older people tend to be richer than younger people), employment (people with jobs are wealthier than people without jobs), and marital status (single people and female-headed households tend to be poorer than homes with a husband and wife). Politicians and the news media are particularly egregious offenders.

Poverty statistics, we should also note, portray only a moment in time. They do not capture the mobility that is available to ambitious and energetic people. A 1995 Census Bureau report noted that while some people remain in poverty for long periods, many more find their status changing year to year. Twenty-one percent of the people who were poor during 1990 were not among the impoverished a year later. Another study, done by the University of Michigan in 1984, found that as many as one-half of the people in poverty escape that condition the following year.[22] "In fact," Michael Tanner writes, "poor Americans are more likely to escape poverty than are their counterparts in many European countries with more extensive social welfare systems."[23] Mobility is what counts.

The point is that the story that government numbers tell about poverty can be highly misleading. The "bottom one-fifth" is populated by different people from year to year. To discuss it as though it were a static group can lead to immense public-policy mischief.

Through the ages there has been little correlation between concern about the poor and the degree of real poverty at the time. There is a tendency to think that if handwringing about the poor increases, there must be more poverty than previously. Not so. A heightened public perception of poverty is entirely consistent with the steady amelioration of the condition of the poor. It is the result of rising expectations. As people's condition improves, they get impatient for even more improvement. Before they grasped what was possible, they were more accepting of their predicament, perhaps believing it was fated and unchangeable.

Alexis de Tocqueville was one of the first to identify this phenomenon. In *The Old Regime and the Revolution*, Tocqueville wrote,

> It is a singular fact that this steadily increasing prosperity [before the French Revolution], far from tranquilizing the population, everywhere promoted a spirit of unrest....
>
> Thus it was precisely in those parts of France where there had been most improvement that popular discontent ran highest. This may seem illogical — but history is full of such paradoxes.[24]

Thus, the lamenting of the poverty problem can intensify at the very time that poverty is becoming less severe. Poverty has been "rediscovered" several times in history, meaning that writers and social activists suddenly began pointing to an allegedly worsening poverty problem in support of their calls for greater government intervention in the marketplace. These rediscoveries were preceded by a spurt in prosperity even among the poorest in society. Moreover, the writers and activists often knew that the poor were better off than before.

For example, concern about poverty increased in late nineteenth-century England. Intellectuals wrote about the poor. Novelists illustrated their plight. Social workers called for reform. Political activists concocted social programs to relieve the disadvantaged. The socialists and welfare statists went on the warpath. Were the poor worse off than previously? Quite the contrary.

Why, then, the acceleration of concern for the poor? Poverty, writes historian Gertrude Himmelfarb, "had become problematic not because it had become worse — on the contrary, the condition of most of the poor, as most contemporaries knew, was better than ever before — but because people had come to believe that it could and should be better than it was."[25] As a result, England enacted welfare-state programs, such as housing assistance, workman's compensation, and health insurance, not to create literal equality but to alleviate poverty.

Political radicals pushed for those measures and others, although, as Himmelfarb writes, "the old article of faith, that the poor were being pauperized, had long been abandoned by most radicals."[26] Study after study detected the general increase in wealth in England from the 1830s to the 1880s, three times faster than the population, according to one report.[27] Economists and statisticians pointed out that the new wealth was reaching the lowest levels of society. Wages were rising and prices were falling. Free trade brought inexpensive imports, and improved mass production made consumer goods available to a wide population — goods that the rich had no access to before.

The champions of the working class acknowledged the material improvement but persisted in their belief that poverty was somehow worse. The statist intellectual J. A. Hobson explained this attitude in 1891: "If by poverty is meant the difference between felt wants and the power to satisfy them, there is more poverty than ever. The income of the poor has grown, but their desires and needs have grown more rapidly.... The poor were once too stupid and too sodden for vigorous discontent; now though their poverty may be less intense, it is more alive, and more militant. The rate of improvement in the condition of the poor is not quick enough to stem the current of its discontent."[28]

If Hobson was right, a perplexing problem arises. The creation of wealth necessarily takes time. It will never be fast enough to keep up with our wants and expectations. Therefore, the very creation of wealth sets in motion political-social sentiments and movements that threaten the process that made affluence possible in the first place. That's a real case of killing the goose that lays the golden egg.

What happened in England also happened in the United States in the nineteenth century. Rising expectations and the visible fortunes of pioneering entrepreneurs created resentment among some who did not make fortunes. Social activists and writers who distrusted the unplanned, "anarchic" nature of capitalism and the pursuit of self-interest found an abundance of apparent justification for government intervention in the economy. The result was a statist mentality that was a departure from an earlier American attitude of distrust of government power. (See chapter 4.)

The intensifying concern about a poverty that was in fact diminishing occurred again after World War II. The end of the war was followed by an explosion of investment and economic growth. As one might expect, society as a whole was getting richer. Charles Murray, in his book *Losing Ground*, shows that from 1950 to 1964 the poverty rate dropped from 30 to 18 percent. Murray writes that "after two decades of reasonably steady progress, improvement slowed in the late sixties and stopped altogether in the seventies."[29] The 1970s are when the Great Society welfare-state programs kicked in with major funding. Thus an increase in poverty coincided with the federal government's battery of programs to end poverty and dependence. "A higher proportion of the American population was officially poor in 1980 than at any time since 1967," Murray writes.[30]

A curious pattern has been identified by economist Thomas Sowell: As society gets richer, there is more notice of the remaining poverty (and an ignorance of the previous drop in poverty). Then as government ostensibly attempts to help the poor, the problem of poverty is aggravated. According to Sowell, government antipoverty programs made more people dependent on government — despite the programs' stated objective of reducing dependency — while spending $5 trillion to the benefit of bureaucrats, politicians, and "private sector" interests who have built careers on the antipoverty crusade.[31]

Today, after all those programs and all those dollars, what are the results? A huge bureaucracy with dozens of programs and a $350 billion annual tab. (Obviously, much of that money does not get to the poor but feeds the bureaucracy and their middle-class suppliers.) Yet there is still a poverty problem, according to the government and the advocates of even more spending. After decades of a war on poverty, the Census Bureau puts the number at 36.5 million (about 13 percent of the population). For the welfare statists, no amount of money is too great. They were especially upset by the 1996 law that ended Aid to Families with Dependent Children, declared welfare not to be a federal entitlement, and mandated that the states limit welfare recipients to five years of benefits and make work a condition for assistance. While there has been some change in attitude toward outright cash welfare and some exodus from the dole, it is premature to say that the welfare state is on the verge of repeal.[32] After all, AFDC was not the only program. There are still housing subsidies, food stamps, education and job-training programs, Medicaid, income supplements, and dozens of other programs — close to eighty major programs in all.

America's cities began to deteriorate in a sea of crime, drug use, illegitimacy, indolence, and dependency *after* the Great Society programs began.[33] That is the legacy of the welfare state and the generous handouts that in some states equated to a job paying $17 an hour.[34] Before the proliferation of welfare programs in the 1960s and 1970s, people were able to walk through inner-city areas safely. Intact families created real neighborhoods, which in turn created security. The contrast with conditions today is stark. Part of the price tag for the welfare state is the utter destruction of many urban areas. (Other programs share the blame, including rent control, business regulations that drive commerce away, incompetent criminal justice, the war on drug users and sellers, and high taxes.)

This discussion is not meant to imply that no one in the United States is in difficult circumstances, long-term or short-term. Of course there are such people, many of them children. Benevolent citizens have compassion for those who have it rough through no fault of their own. No decent person takes joy from the suffering of innocents. The libertarian simply believes that it is illegitimate to *force* people to render assistance.

Yes, there is a small number of genuinely poor people. But in most discussions about how to eradicate poverty, it is often forgotten that it is not poverty that needs explaining. Mankind was born into poverty. Poverty was man's lot for thousands of year. Subsistence and short life spans were the norm. As darkness is the absence of light, so poverty is the absence of wealth. It is the default condition.

Thus, what requires explanation is wealth. Wealth is unnatural. If we wish to truly understand poverty, we should study the creation of wealth and the conditions that make it possible. Government can block routes out of poverty. Minimum wage laws and other labor legislation, taxes on employment (such as mandated working conditions), general taxation, occupational licensing, and myriad other restrictions increase the difficulty of digging out of poverty. That is not to say that self-help is impossible; people in bad circumstances better themselves every day. But government indisputably makes it harder, especially for people who are the least skilled at navigating the bureaucratic shoals.

With the dramatic growth of wealth in the nineteenth century, many people have gotten the idea that the problem of production has been solved. It was as if the economy were now a perpetual-motion machine, or, at worst, an engine that only needs to be tended by a caring government. All that remained was to find the best means of distributing the wealth. Distribution was regarded as unrelated to production. Hence, the various schemes to transfer wealth from one group to another. Such thinking vastly changed thinking about the political system in this country and other market-oriented countries. This picture of production and distribution is found, for instance, in the work of John Stuart Mill, the sometime-defender of classical liberal ideas.

101

The fallacy should be obvious. The economic system is not a machine, much less one of the perpetual-motion variety. Yet our language is full of metaphors that impute machinelike characteristics to the economy. We are warned that it might overheat or cool down; the Federal Reserve System is said to control the throttle, and so on. In reality, the economy is a human process. People act under certain conditions to achieve their objectives. They coordinate their activities with others, respond to price signals, and act on incentives — all in order to obtain the goods they want. Their success is not guaranteed. Things are changing all the time. Moreover, nothing ensures that they will continue to exert the effort they exerted in the past. If the government enacts a program to "distribute" wealth according to its own formula, it will tend to discourage production and yield less wealth than otherwise would have been created. So how can the problem of production be regarded as solved?

It is fallacious to look at production and distribution as separate parts of economic activity. They are two parts of the same activity. To be more precise, in a market, there is no *distribution*. If Jones produces a toaster and trades it to Smith for a book, the toaster has not been distributed. The producer/owner decided to exchange it for something he valued more.

To talk about distribution is to talk as though unowned goods magically appear without anyone's exerting effort. An anointed authority now has to decide how to distribute them. He may use a fair or unfair standard. But however he chooses, the good cannot be claimed on the basis of who produced and therefore owned them. It is as if *no one* produced them.

That is not how goods come into existence. The production of goods is necessarily governed by property titles, contracts, and agreements that *in advance* settle the question of who owns them once they are completed. At the simplest end, if Jones on his own time whittles a wood sculpture with his knife and his piece of wood, it is his and his alone. He can choose to keep it, give it away, or find a willing buyer. There is no distribution stage. More complicated production arrangements don't change the elements of the story. At the end of the production stage, there is an owner or owners who have the right to decide how the goods will be disposed. Therefore, in a market where property titles are legitimate and protected, there can be no unjust "distribution." If someone disposes of a product without the permission of the owner, that is not distribution. It is theft.

Ignorance of this point leads to policies that threaten everyone's well-being. If government uses its power to determine how goods will be handed out, it will adversely influence production in the future. It is shortsighted to look only at the goods already produced. Production is a continuing process. In the extreme, people are not likely to continue producing only to see their goods confiscated by the government. (The famines induced by Stalin and Mao were the direct result of the confiscation of the crops of farmers, who stopped producing.) Lesser forms of confiscation, for example, taxes on incomes, have only a less dramatic effect on the incentive to produce. It is likely that at some point people work less when they cannot reap the benefits of their effort.

The upshot is that if distribution is treated as separate from production, there will be less and less to distribute. We have not entered an era of superabundance, where we need have no concern about production. Scarcity is still the rule of nature and human nature. We always want more of the things we value than we can have at any moment. While goods are more plentiful and cheaper than previously, that is the result not of a perpetual-motion machine but of human effort and ingenuity under certain conditions and incentives. Given the right conditions, wealth will grow in the future. But given the wrong conditions, wealth can contract. The problem of production is never solved once and for all. It has to be solved every day. The implications for the poor should be evident. A contraction of wealth would take its greatest toll on those who have little to begin with.

In economic terms, dividing production and distribution leads to a loss of wealth and to more poverty. In moral terms, it leads to a loss of individual rights and civility. A civil society is one in which people are respected in their rights. When the government presumes to distribute what someone else has produced, it undermines civil society and introduces barbarity. The disparaging of property rights cultivates covetousness and leads to wider infringements on liberty. Once wealth is seen as a common holding, ideas on how to dispose of it will proliferate. The scope of government will grow, and the incentive to produce will diminish. The anti-property ethic even makes street crime more common, as people cease to believe that others have a right to be secure in their possessions.

It should be easy to see that the poor have no long-term interest in the view that production and distribution should be separated. In relative terms, the poor stand the most to gain from economic growth. When the Industrial Revolution got under way, those with low incomes benefited greatly, even disproportionately compared with the wealthy of the day. Production shifted from goods for the elite to goods for the masses. That is one reason why the period was so revolutionary. Within a short period of time, people who were not rich could own more than one outfit of clothes and other items that previously were accessible only to the rich. Likewise, an expansion of production today would disproportionately benefit lower-income people. More goods mean lower prices and wider choice.

There is a sense in which the problem of production has been solved. It is true in the sense that we understand — or should understand by now — the conditions that enable us to maximize the production of wealth. Even a casual study of events in the communist world reveal that the key to prosperity is individual freedom, including secure property rights, the rule of law, and limitations on the power of government.[35] The connection between freedom and prosperity is too obvious to need lengthy documentation. It should not be necessary to point out, for the umpteenth time, the contrasts between East and West Germany, North and South Korea, and China and Taiwan or Hong Kong.

This leads to an answer to the question: Don't we owe something to the poor? Yes, we do. We owe the poor the same thing we owe everyone else: respect for individual rights. We owe it to the poor to remove the welfare state tethers that hold them back and that siphon off the productive energy of capitalism: the minimum wage, which destroys jobs; rent control, which destroys housing; union laws, which protect high-skilled workers at the expense of low-skilled workers; building codes and zoning, which increase the price of homes; Social Security, Medicare, and Medicaid, which consume savings; welfare, which induces idleness, illegitimacy, and an impoverished state of mind. The list goes on and on. All those government programs are justified in terms of the welfare of the people. But all of them hurt people and make them poorer than they'd be otherwise.

The free market not only raises living standards by expanding production, it also cultivates virtue. Take away paternalistic government and people will more readily see the value of industry, integrity, honesty, decency, responsibility, foresight, and the other habits of mind that make the good life possible. Reality and the market are great teachers.

But what of the "safety net"? Since the nineteenth century, we have been so propagandized by the welfare statists that the term "safety net" now only means the web of paternalistic government programs. But there is another safety net that has gone unnoticed. It is privately provided, and it includes charitable organizations, fraternal associations, and insurance companies. The Red Cross, the Salvation Army, and the United Way are part of this safety net (to the extent they do not receive taxpayer money). But so are the profit-making companies that provide all manner of insurance.[36]

In other words, advocating the repeal of the welfare state does not stem from disapproval of people's banding together to help each other when in distress. The issue is freedom versus force. Voluntary mutual aid is inherent in freedom. (This is a distinction lost on President Clinton, who a few years ago said that while "the era of big government is over," we would not return to the days when people "fended for themselves.")

The private charitable sector in the United States is huge, and it undoubtedly would be larger if government were to leave this field, repeal taxes, and let people decide how to spend their own money. Government welfare spending tends to reduce private giving.[37] When the public believe welfare spending is being cut, as they did (though erroneously) during the Reagan years, they increase their contributions.[38] That's part of the answer to those who believe private charity cannot raise enough money for the destitute. The other part is that in a truly free economy, the number of people needing help would be far smaller.

According to the Census Bureau, 1994 cash contributions from all private sources totaled roughly $260 billion.[39] If cash contributions and time volunteered are counted, Americans donate some $300 billion a year to charitable causes; that doesn't count informal aid.[40] Private charity has virtues that government programs cannot approach: individual flexibility, assistance targeted to greatest need, and efficiency. By contrast, "Today, 70 cents of every dollar goes, not to poor people," Michael Tanner writes, "but to government bureaucrats and others who serve the poor."[41] Moreover, private charity will tend to have an interest in inculcating independence in the people it is helping in order to make any assistance temporary.

But charity is not the only or even the main way that people, including lower-income people, would be protected against misfortune. We can say this with confidence because the United States (and England) has had ample experience with what was called mutual aid.[42] In nineteenth-century America a vast private fraternal insurance movement — a working-class movement — began providing millions of Americans — especially blacks and immigrants — with life insurance and protection against income loss from sickness and accident. Some fraternal organizations even operated proto–

health maintenance organizations.

The fraternals, which were decentralized membership organizations, or lodges, were an outgrowth of the British friendly societies, the medieval guilds, and the ancient burial societies. Often organized along racial and ethnic lines, these organizations found success in the insurance field because their small size and homogeneity gave them advantages over commercial insurers; since the members knew each other, had continuing associations, and looked to the organization for other services, the fraternals could cope better with standard insurance problems such as moral hazard and adverse selection. Familiarity bred honor. Taking benefits under false pretenses cheated one's own friends. ("Moral hazard" refers to the complacency that insurance can create and the increased likelihood of an event's happening *because* it is insured against. "Adverse selection" refers to a preponderance among insurance customers of those likely to make claims.)

Before the Great Depression, mutual-aid organizations were a significant source of "social security," second only to the churches. The organizations had eighteen million members in 1920, almost 30 percent of all adults over twenty. Lodges, some of them secret societies, were central institutions in urban neighborhoods and small towns throughout the United States. The Masons and Odd Fellows built old-age homes for their members and provided other forms of assistance.

The explicit fraternal insurance societies had a bigger social impact than the lodges. Their principal protection came through a form of life insurance, the "death benefit," which was paid to beneficiaries of the deceased. The societies also paid sick benefits. The larger societies, affiliated with the National Fraternal Congress, paid an average death benefit of $1,100, which was roughly about what the average American worker earned in 1919. A study of wage earners in Chicago in 1919 showed that 74.8 percent of husbands had life insurance. Half of those policies were from fraternal orders. Elderly members could cash in the value of their insurance, and they often used the money to start businesses. In 1931, at least nine million mostly working-class people had fraternal insurance. (By contrast, 93,000 families were receiving state mothers' pensions.)

In the early 1900s many fraternal societies started providing formal health and accident insurance. By 1920 sickness benefits included the care of a doctor, who contracted with the fraternal societies and charged lower rates than doctors did for traditional fee-for-service. House calls were often included. Organized medicine did not like the practice — some doctors found it an undesirable form of competition that depressed incomes — and the state medical societies and state regulators tried to stop it. "By the 1910s, doctors had launched an all-out war against lodge practice," writes historian David T. Beito. "Throughout the country, medical associations imposed a range of sanctions against lodge doctors, including expulsion from the association and denial of hospital facilities.... By the end of the 1930s, the once vibrant health care alternative of lodge practice, which less than two decades before had inspired trepidation throughout the medical establishment, had virtually disappeared."[43]

The fraternal societies were particularly effective at serving blacks, immigrants, and women. In 1919, more than 93 percent of black families in Chicago had life insurance. In contrast to today's welfare system, mutual aid had a strong moral component because, by its very nature, help from a fraternal society aimed at fostering moral values such as independence, self-reliance, and foresight. The reciprocal nature of fraternal societies enabled them to avoid treating aid either as an entitlement or as demeaning charity. As government relief became more dominant, those involved with fraternal societies grasped the difference in the service provided and feared for the future.

The number of National Fraternal Congress societies peaked in 1925 (120,000), then leveled off and declined. During the Depression, the decline increased slightly and then accelerated after World War II. Surely it is no coincidence that government, first at the state level then at the federal level, moved into the welfare business during that time. Before the New Deal, many states had workers' compensation and mothers' pension systems. When workers' compensation began in the 1910s and 1920s, employee fraternal organizations that had provided accident insurance for factory workers withdrew from the workplace. In the 1930s, the federal government initiated Social Security and Aid to Dependent Children (later called Aid to Families with Dependent Children). Obviously, such programs would depress the demand for fraternal insurance.

It is reasonable to speculate that the government safety net has crowded out voluntary private activities aimed at providing similar services. Citizens were taxed to support government programs, which appeared to perform the same functions as services for which one had to pay extra. Yet while private solutions stressed reciprocity and independence, government programs since the 1960s have promoted "entitlements" and fostered dependence.[44] Moreover, private solutions were varied and flexible almost beyond imagination. In contrast, government "solutions" are usually one-size-fits-all — or, rather, no one.

In other words, bad safety nets drive out good safety nets.

What about the poor? In a free society, in which all kinds of voluntary, creative activities may go on unimpeded by government, the actual poor would be far fewer and they would be far better off than today. A free society is not utopia. Nevertheless, hard-headed realism and history teach us that compulsion in the name of humanitarianism is self-defeating and that liberty is effective. The poor have the most to gain from abolition of the welfare state.

Notes

[1] Adam Smith, *The Theory of Moral Sentiments* (1759; Indianapolis: Liberty Classics, 1976).

[2] David Hume, *Hume's Moral and Political Philosophy,* ed. Henry D. Aiken (New York: Hafner Publishing Co., 1948), containing *A Treatise of Human Nature,* part 2, *Of Justice and Injustice,* chapter 1, "Justice, Whether a Natural or Artificial Virtue?" p. 52.

[3] The handwriting is on the wall. Congress authorized the Federal Communications Commission to begin taxing telephone users to finance Internet connections to schools, libraries, and health facilities, all for $4.9 billion in 1998. See James K. Glassman, "A New Tax for a New Year," *Washington Post,* December 2, 1997, p. A27.

[4] See generally Gordon Tullock, *Welfare for the Well-To-Do* (Dallas: The Fisher Institute, 1983) and William C. Mitchell and Randy T. Simmons, *Beyond Politics: Markets, Welfare, and the Failure of Bureaucracy* (Boulder, Colo.: Westview Press, 1994).

[5] Lawrence E. Harrison, *Underdevelopment Is a State of Mind: The Latin American Case* (Lanham, Md.: University Press of America, 1985).

[6] Richard Vedder and Lowell Gallaway, "The War on the Poor," Institute for Policy Innovation, Lewisville, Tex., June 1992; cited in Michael Tanner, *The End of Welfare: Fighting Poverty in the Civil Society* (Washington, D.C.: Cato Institute, 1996), p. 28.

[7] See James Payne, "Why the War on Poverty Failed," *The Freeman: Ideas on Liberty,* January 1999, pp. 6–10, and Dale E. Walsh, "Character and Government Policy," *The Freeman: Ideas on Liberty,* July 1998, pp. 394–97.

[8] Alan Reynolds, "Economic Foundations of the American Dream" in *The New Promise of American Life,* ed. Lamar Alexander and Chester Finn (Indianapolis: Hudson Institute, 1995), p. 214.

[9] See David Kelley, *A Life of One's Own: Individual Rights and the Welfare State* (Washington, D.C.: Cato Institute, 1998), pp. 15–29. On the corruption of the concept of freedom as "freedom from want," see James Bovard, *Freedom in Chains: The Rise of the State and the Demise of the Citizen* (New York: St. Martin's Press, 1999), pp. 66–77.

[10] Tanner, p. 6.

[11] See http://www.census.gov/hhes/income/income97/ prs98asc.html (September 24, 1998).

[12] Tanner, p. 9.

[13] See http://www.census.gov/hhes/income/income97/prs98asc.html.

[14] Henry Hazlitt, *The Conquest of Poverty* (1972; Irvington-on-Hudson, N.Y.: The Foundation for Economic Education, 1996), p. 33.

[15] The term "distribution" can be misleading. It is meant here on in a statistical sense. In a market-oriented economy, incomes are not distributed in the way that parents distribute allowances to children.

[16] W. Michael Cox and Richard Alm, "Time Well Spent: The Declining *Real* Cost of Living in America," 1997 Annual Report, Federal Reserve Bank of Dallas, p. 3. Also see their book, *Myths of Rich and Poor: We're Better Off Than We Think* (New York: Basic Books, 1999).

[17] Cox and Alm, "Time Well Spent," p. 4.

[18] Quoted in Gertrude Himmelfarb, *The Idea of Poverty: England in the Early Industrial Revolution* (New York: Alfred A. Knopf, 1983), p. 531.

[19] Bruce Bartlett, "How Poor Are the Poor?" *The American Enterprise,* January/February 1996, pp. 58–59.

[20] Ibid. Noncash government benefits, such as food stamps and housing subsidies, also lead to an understatement of income.

[21] See Barbara Vobejda and Judith Havemann, "Welfare Clients Already Work, Off the Books," *Washington Post,* November 3, 1997, p. A1. A year after the 1996 welfare reform, which included a work requirement and a five-year limit on benefits, about a million recipients left the dole and presumably found jobs. Barbara Vobejda and Jon Jeter, "True Test of Reform Just Starting," *Washington Post,* August 22, 1997, p. A13. At the end of 1998, the federal government said that 28 percent of adults in the welfare system were in full-time or part-time jobs. Under the rules of the 1996 welfare reform, which abolished welfare as an entitlement, 25 percent were to be working in 1998. By 2002, half of the adults on the welfare rolls are to have a job. Robert Pear, "Most States Meet Work Requirement of Welfare Law," *New York Times,* December 30, 1998.

[22] Tanner summarizes the studies in *The End of Welfare,* p. 10.

[23] Ibid., p. 11.

[24] Quoted in Hazlitt, *The Conquest of Poverty,* p. 129.

[25] Gertrude Himmelfarb, *Poverty and Compassion: The Moral Imagination of the Late Victorians* (New York: Alfred A. Knopf, 1991), p. 12.

[26] Ibid., pp. 32–33.

[27] Ibid., p. 25.

[28] Quoted in ibid., p. 32.

[29] Charles Murray, *Losing Ground: American Social Policy, 1950–1980* (New York: Basic Books, 1984), p. 58.

[30] Ibid., p. 58.

[31] Thomas Sowell, *The Vision of the Anointed: Self-Congratulation as a Basis for Social Policy* (New York: Basic Books, 1995), pp. 12–13. See also James Payne, *Overcoming Welfare: Expecting More from the Poor and from Ourselves* (New York: Basic Books, 1998) and Payne, "Why the War on Poverty Failed."

[32] The federal government announced that as of fall 1998, the number of people on welfare was its lowest in thirty years: eight million. The decline was slowing, however. See Laura Meckler, "Welfare Roll Numbers Hit 30-Year Low," *Washington Post,* January 25, 1999, p. A4.

[32] See Tanner's appendix, pp. 185–217. See also James L. Payne, "Welfare 'Cuts'?" *The American Enterprise,* November/December 1997, pp. 38–41.

[33] Tanner, pp. 69–94.

[34] Ibid., pp. 66–67.

[35] That list is redundant: "private property" says it all. Thanks to Israel Kirzner for this point.

[36] The Amish have a well-developed private safety net. See Hannah Lapp, "Life Without Uncle Sam," *The American Enterprise,* November/December 1997, pp. 28–31.

[37] Tanner, pp. 145–46.

[38] Ibid., p. 145.

[39] *The American Almanac, 1996–1997* (Washington, D.C.: Bureau of the Census, 1996), p. 388.

[40] Ibid., p. 134.

[41] The estimate was made by Robert Woodson and is cited in Tanner, p. 136.

[42] This discussion is drawn from David T. Beito, "Mutual Aid for Social Welfare: The Case of American Fraternal Societies," *Criti-*

cal Review 4 (Fall 1990) and David Green, *Reinventing Civil Society: The Rediscovery of Welfare without Politics* (London: IEA Health and Welfare Unit, 1993).

[43] David T. Beito, "Lodge Doctors and the Poor," in *Private Means, Public Ends: Voluntarism vs. Coercion,* ed. J. Wilson Mixon Jr. (Irvington-on-Hudson, N.Y.: The Foundation for Economic Education, 1996), p. 95. See also David T. Beito, *From Mutual Aid to the Welfare State, Fraternal Societies and Social Services, 1890–1967* (Chapel Hill, N.C.: University of North Carolina Press, 2000), which was released as the present book was being prepared for printing.

[44] See Marvin Olasky, *The Tragedy of American Compassion* (Washington, D.C.: Regnery/Gateway, 1992) for a discussion of these issues, including the distinction made by mutual aid between the deserving and undeserving poor. For the story on how mutual-aid societies helped bring their own demise by lobbying the federal government in 1893, see John Chodes, "Friendly Societies: Voluntary Social Security — and More," in Mixon, pp. 81–86.

6

Time to Abolish the Welfare State

T he welfare state exists to transfer resources from those who produced them to those who did not. There can be countless motives for effecting a transfer: to equalize incomes; to feed and house the poor; to eradicate drug use; to promote exports; to inhibit imports; to subsidize business and agriculture; to certify the safety of food, medicines, toys, and appliances; to make buildings sturdy; to discourage smoking or drinking; to preserve wetlands and animal habitats; to ensure retirement income; to guarantee safety in the workplace; to advance research; to educate children; to provide affordable medical care; to control rents; to end racial discrimination; to plan residential development.

Whenever the state attempts to do those things, by definition it accumulates and exercises power. The power of government always comes down to physical force. Someone is either compelled to do something he wishes not to do, whether it is paying taxes or complying with decrees, or stopped from engaging in the peaceful pursuit of his choice.

When politicians want to bestow largess, they and the aspiring recipients are wont to talk about rights, or entitlements. Political activists and social philosophers declare that all have the right to a living wage or to decent housing or to quality medical care. Such talk may be well-intentioned, but it is wrong just the same. The consequences for liberty and real welfare are perilous.

Take, for example, the idea of a right to medical care — a classic counterfeit right. A counterfeit right is any claim expressed as a right that would expand the power of the state at the expense of genuine rights. The "right to medical care" is alluring. People not used to dissecting political discourse will think of the benefits of having medical services provided "free" or at a guaranteed low price. More sophisticated people may see the proposal as a giant insurance system and feel that there can be no danger in it. If all citizens pay and all have access to care when they need it, what could be wrong?

Much could be wrong. First, for a right to be real, it has to be capable of being exercised without anyone's affirmative cooperation. The full exercise of my right over my person (self-ownership) requires you to do *nothing* except *refrain* from killing, assaulting, or otherwise physically harming me. The full exercise of my property rights requires you to do *nothing* except *refrain* from taking what is mine. You have no positive enforceable obligations to me apart from any you accept through your consent.

That principle of nonobligation is an excellent test to which we can submit any proffered "right." How does the right to medical care hold up? Leaving aside self-treatment, it is difficult to see how there can be such a right. Medical care, unlike air, is not superabundant. It is produced by other people who spent money and exerted effort to acquire expertise. It requires the use of instruments and drugs, which have to be manufactured by others. A right to those products and services necessarily implies the right to compel others to provide them. But that would make slaves of those so compelled. What of their rights?

Since the "right to medical care" requires an affirmative obligation on the part of others, it fails the rights test. Simply put, that "right" cannot coexist with the right of others to be left alone.

In today's welfare state, doctors, nurses, and manufacturers of medical instruments and pharmaceuticals are not typically forced to provide their services at gunpoint. So this critique may not seem germane. But although providers are not directly compelled, the taxpayers are. Taxation is somewhat less egregious than conscription, but it is still compulsion; the penalty for not complying includes fines, confiscation of property, imprisonment, even death. (That's no exaggeration. If a citizen refuses to pay and attempts to defend his property, officers of the state are authorized to use deadly force.) Taking people's earnings is tantamount to taking their time and labor.[1] Since the compulsion of taxation is spread across large numbers of people and leaves them free to choose how they make a living, it seems less offensive than conscription of medical personnel. But it doesn't fundamentally change what's going on. Someone is being forced to provide something to someone else without a freely accepted contractual obligation to provide it. The fact that those who are taxed also are beneficiaries of coercively financed services does not alter the principle.

Thus the right to medical care, like all counterfeit rights, fails on at least one rather important count: it cannot be a right because it must negate the real rights of others. The purpose of rights is to enable human beings to live like the potentially rational beings they are. To live that way, conflict over the use of resources must be averted. People need to know what they may and may not do with respect to physical objects. A distinctly human life is impossible in a Hobbesian war of all against all. Life is the fundamental value that makes the very idea of value possible, and life comes in units known as individuals. Rights are a moral concept that enables individuals to live and prosper.[2]

"Welfare rights" such as the right to medical care undermine bona fide rights in ways other than coercing taxpayers. Imagine for a moment a right to apples. That may sound nice, but an immediate problem arises. How many apples does each of us have a right to? Scarcity is the natural condition, which means that at any given moment our wishes exceed supply. (Freedom has a knack for loosening nature's initially strict bonds of scarcity.) Declaring such a right would quickly empty the shelves of apples, making a mockery of our "right." Nor would the shelves soon be replenished, for who would produce apples if we all have a right to them, that is, the right to appropriate them without paying?

We might decide to trust people to take only what they need. But that doesn't get us far. Even if we assume a population of self-effacing people, "need," in this context, is subjective. You can live without apples; so in a strict sense, you need none. But if we expand the concept of "need" a little, we open the gates to endless disagreement over who needs how many apples. I may think I need many more than you need and vice versa. There is no way to resolve a dispute of that nature. The state could ration apples. We could trust the government to scientifically determine how many apples each of us needs. If you believe that, you will also believe that the ruling party won't manage to get more apples than the rest of us. The point is that what started out as a "right" ends up as an expansion of state power.

Now substitute medical care for apples. Government control

in the name of a right to apples might be no more than an inconvenience. Government control in the name of medical care would be downright deadly. Yet what is the alternative once a right to medical care is declared? There is no way everyone can have all the medical care they would want if it is (that is, appears to be) costless or nearly so. The demand for resources exceeds supply. The government will decide who gets what.

Thus the right to medical care must mean — no exceptions — the power of government, in principle, to determine who gets how much medical care and who does not. Government is in the triage business. It may not exercise that power immediately. But given the economics of the matter, sooner or later it will. That has nothing to do with freedom and rights and everything to do with control, literally, of people's lives.

I do not exaggerate. A major ethical issue these days involves the "right to die," or the misnamed right to "assisted suicide."[3] That is overshadowing one that may be more consequential, the so-called "duty to die." Some years ago, Colorado's governor, Richard Lamm, argued that old people should know when it is time to quit this earth in favor of younger people. (The civil libertarian Nat Hentoff wrote recently that Lamm is, inexplicably, a devotee of exercise, presumably to lengthen his life.) John Hardwig, a medical ethicist and social philosopher, agrees.

We need not address whether an old person should preserve his heirs' inheritance rather than spend it on medical care. For the time being, that is a private, not a political, matter of how one spends one's own money. (The inheritance tax could have consequences for such a decision.) What is relevant is how that ethical issue is transformed when government controls medical spending in the name of "the right to health care." The Lamm-Hardwig position would be translated into a rather unpleasant public policy: the withholding of care for the elderly in the name of the wise allocation of resources and "making room" for the young. (Elderly leaders no doubt would be excepted.) As a matter of public policy, might not the politicians and bureaucrats decide that heart transplants, knee replacements, and mastectomies for octogenarians are a waste of money that could be used to treat younger people whose productive years lie ahead? This sort of thing is not considered beyond the pale in the increasingly fragile welfare states of western Europe.

If government pays for medical care, such public policies are inevitable. Money is limited. The presumption will be that "government money" should be spent wisely and not squandered. Tough choices will have to be made. Politicians and bureaucrats will make them. (The alternative, as President Clinton said, is to hope that the American people spend their money "right.")

What starts as the right to medical care ends as the authority of the state to say who lives with and without pain, indeed, who lives and who dies. So it goes with all counterfeit "welfare rights." As Bertrand de Jouvenel said, "The more one considers the matter, the clearer it becomes that redistribution is in effect far less a redistribution of free income from the richer to the poorer, as we have imagined, than a redistribution of power from the individual to the state."[4]

Since the welfare state is built on such devices that increase the power of government at the expense of the liberty of individuals, it contradicts basic moral precepts. The issue isn't whether people ought, in some sense, to donate money to good causes. It is rather whether they should be *legally compelled* to do so. Who would have the state compel everything that "ought" to be done?

The welfare state also conflicts with the American rationale for government. The Declaration of Independence asserts the unalienable rights to life, liberty, and the pursuit happiness and then points out that "to secure these Rights, Governments are instituted among Men, deriving their just Powers from the Consent of the Governed." Thomas Jefferson's Declaration goes on: "Whenever any Form of Government becomes destructive of these Ends, it is the Right of the People to alter or to abolish it, and to institute new Government, laying its Foundation on such Principles, and organizing its Powers in such Form, as to them shall seem most likely to effect their Safety and Happiness."[5]

As noted in chapter 1, the U.S. Constitution set up a national government with a few delegated powers. Its silence on a matter was to indicate the denial of federal power in that matter. The delegated powers are found in Article I, Section 8. Starkly missing from that list is the power to transfer wealth from one person to another. That should dispose of the matter. But the issue was hammered home in the Bill of Rights, where the Fifth Amendment forbids, among other things, the taking of private property "for public use without just compensation."[6]

A full discussion of the "takings" clause would be too much of a digression here. But a few points are relevant. The clause, unfortunately, authorizes the government to violate individual liberty, since under eminent domain officials can compel a person to sell his property. But the Framers at least were aware of the potential for abuse that the state always poses. That skepticism about power led them to put restrictions in the takings clause. First, property could be taken only for "public use." The phrase is vague. But the intention is clear: the government should not be allowed to take the property of one citizen merely to give it to another. Some general benefit must be the objective. (They had in mind what today we call "public goods," the kind of goods, theoretically, that benefit all and are difficult to charge individual users for.[7])

Second, the Framers required that owners be justly compensated. That requirement has problems, too. In the marketplace we know what just compensation is. It is the price consented to by seller and buyer. But under a forced sale, no price paid can be considered just because consent is lacking. The government must resort to inferior proxies, such as the price paid for "comparable" properties. A "comparable" is never identical. The precise value of a thing to a person is not intrinsic, but rather "subjective," in the sense that its importance has much to do with his particular circumstances and objectives. But like the "public use" criterion, the requirement of just compensation has two notable features: It recognizes that a property owner is not a mere servant of the state. If the government wants his property, it has to pay him something. (More precisely, it forces the taxpayers to compensate him.) Moreover, the compensation requirement to some extent restrains the government by presenting it with tradeoffs. Obviously, if private property is free for the taking, the government will take much more than if it has to spend tax revenues for it.

Legal scholar Richard Epstein, in his close study of the takings clause, concludes that the welfare state suffers "fatal constitutional infirmities" because transfer programs do not meet the criteria of public use and just compensation. The recipients are private parties and the taxpayers are uncompensated. The argument that taxpayers are compensated "in kind," that is, they benefit from the civil peace that aid to the poor ensures, is a spurious rationalization.[8]

Thus the welfare state is immoral and unconstitutional. As indicated earlier, it also is destructive of processes that create wealth and prosperity.[9] Why then did America turn to the welfare state from its individualist and libertarian origins? That is a complex question with a large range of correct answers. Some were discussed in chapter 4. Moreover, it is surely the case that people, wishing to economize on their scarce time and effort, look for the path of least resistance. If they can get what they want through political transfers, many people are happy to do so. Collecting tax-financed benefits doesn't feel like receiving stolen property, although that's what it is. As we saw in chapter 2, the political process is subject to mystification: payments are hidden and disconnected from benefits; production is uncoupled from consumption.[10] The idea of entitlement has been corrupted.[11] Citizens find themselves in a seemingly amoral arena in which they might as well get what they can before someone else takes it. In the animal jungle the rule is eat or be eaten. In the political jungle it's subsidize or be subsidized.[12]

The welfare state also has origins in envy, the virulent disposition that induces people not only to want the kind of things that others have, but to want others to be deprived of those very things. H. L. Mencken wrote that "there is only one sound argument for democracy, and that is the argument that it is a crime for any man to hold himself out as better than other men, and, above all, a most heinous offense for him to prove it."[13] When the first fortunes were being made in the Industrial Revolution, they undoubtedly engendered resentment among some people. Although for the first time in history, those fortunes were built largely by producing for mass consumption, it was tempting for people to believe the wealthy profited at their expense. That made them easy marks for demagogues lusting for power. In his classic study of envy, Helmut Schoeck commented that democracy, and by implication the welfare state, needs the "envy-motive" because it gives weak political candidates the chance to sound as though they can accomplish something. "Anybody, once in office, can confiscate or destroy," Schoeck wrote.[14]

It is interesting to ask why the wealth of kings never inspired the same resentment as the wealth of entrepreneurs. Bertrand de Jouvenel suggests that it was one thing for "my ruler" to be rich; quite another when the wealthy came from humble circumstances like nearly everyone else. That was an affront, and therefore suspect.[15]

We know why the nobility in England resented the rise of capitalism. The erosion of class distinctions was disconcerting and threatening. Common folk could have things, such as an expansive wardrobe, that previously only the wealthy could afford. That's not quite accurate. They could have *better* things. While America had no traditional nobility, it is surely true that what passed for an aristocracy here was uncomfortable with the social mobility that capitalism produced. "A characteristic feature of the unhampered market society is that it is no respecter of vested interests," wrote Ludwig von Mises.[16] Free markets do nothing to keep people "in their place."

Another motive propelling the welfare state was insecurity

about change and ignorance of the future. One's economic position ultimately depends on the tastes and preferences of free and fickle consumers.[17] Someone making a high income today can be living paycheck to paycheck tomorrow — and vice versa. No one is guaranteed a particular position in the marketplace. The specter of failure always hovers. Knowledge is limited. Change is the unchanging rule. That can be discomfiting. But there is a bright side. "In an unhampered market economy the absence of security, i.e., the absence of protection for vested interests, is the principle that makes for a steady improvement in material well-being," Mises wrote.[18] The freedom that permits change and failure is also what makes innovation, discovery, and inventiveness possible. Those things improve everyone's welfare.

The welfare statists' fallacy is that in a free market, people have no way to create security. In fact, they have many ways. In chapter 5 we saw how a free society can provide classic "welfare" services, such as sickness and accident insurance, through mutual-aid organizations and profit-making firms. Unemployment insurance could also be provided by entrepreneurs (although savings is the traditional hedge against unemployment). Let's look at another area in which the marketplace can provide what the welfare state purports to provide: consumer protection.

Today the Consumer Product Safety Commission, the Food and Drug Administration, and the Federal Trade Commission are charged with protecting consumers from shoddy, ineffective, and dangerous products. But there is overwhelming evidence that government "protection" is inferior to market protection. Varying Gresham's Law, bad protection drives out good. When the government assures citizens it is taking care of them, they let their guard down. Safety is removed from the competitive realm because all products have the same alleged guarantor, the state. Consumers are given a false sense of security, which, I submit, is worse than no sense of security at all. For example, firms that satisfy government standards are regarded as a homogeneous class, although the safety of their products may in fact differ greatly. Think of all those savings-and-loans that had the same FSLIC sticker on their windows. The consumers' power of discrimination is dulled by the fallback: "They couldn't sell (or do) that if it wasn't safe."[19] Individual firms have no incentive to break out of the pack on the safety issue.

Economist Randall Holcombe notes that government regulation interferes with self-regulation in another way. If the government leaves an industry unregulated, it insidiously lulls consumers into complacency. After all, if there was something to worry about, the government would be regulating the industry. "With this illusion of a government umbrella protecting everyone from harm," Holcombe writes, "there is relatively little public demand for private regulation."[20]

As Milton and Rose Friedman point out, generally speaking, the most effective protector of the consumer is the competitive market itself.[21] Firms wish to stay in business and expand their clientele. Thus they try to please their customers. They strive for good reputations and goodwill.[22] The role of brand names is obvious in this connection. A brand name is shorthand for a company's history of quality. Occasional stories of consumer rip-offs stand out in our memories precisely because they are the exception. The more normal situation — where a product is faithfully represented — is hardly noticed because it is commonplace. The system is not perfect. But it beats any alternative. We must judge the market against real-world government regulation, not an idealized construct. Experience and public-choice theory have demonstrated that the government does not come through that comparison unscathed. There is no reason to think that bureaucrats have better foresight or information than business people. On the contrary, as the Friedmans and others have pointed out, firms that make errors can go out of business; not so governments. Moreover, government mistakes may be harder to discern. Bureaucrats, fearing responsibility for a product that does harm, tend to be overcautious and err on the side of withholding products — including potentially life-saving products — from the market. Since the products don't appear, consumers are not likely to be aware that the government is responsible for the consequences that would have been averted had the products been brought to market.

Consumers are also protected by various middlemen, the retailers who would suffer consumer wrath if they sell poor products. They thus have a strong interest in filtering out shoddy merchandise. (Of course, the laws regarding liability and fraud also play a role in consumer protection, but I am concentrating here on prospective protection.)

Another protection for consumers is the market for product information. *Consumer Reports* and *Consumer Research* are two old magazines that test products and sell their findings to subscribers. Both have carefully guarded their good names, and neither has been suspected of corruption. Specialized publications rate automobiles, stereo equipment, personal computers, software, and so on. The incentive to be objective is obvious. Competition for reputation and

121

goodwill applies as much to the purveyors of consumer information as to manufacturers. Their customers are free to take their business elsewhere.

The market for information can take many forms. Think of what *60 Minutes* and other television magazine programs have done over the years in exposing dishonest operations. Of course, occasionally, as with NBC's *Dateline* program about a GM vehicle, they do a hatchet job. But that is unusual and the market has methods of self-correction.

The history of private product certification is quite rich. In contrast to the testers at *Consumer Reports*, many private certifiers test products for and at the expense of manufacturers. Products that satisfy certain standards may display the certifier's seal of approval. That seal is valuable only to the extent that the issuer has a reputation for objectivity and high standards. Rumors that a certifier can be "bought" would be fatal. The value of its seal would plummet to zero.

Underwriters Laboratories is a prime example of a private certifier. On the strength of its reputation and without coercive power, it encourages companies to meet its exacting standards for electrical appliances and other goods. When UL approves a product, the organization uses various methods, all contractually accepted, to ensure that the product continues to meet standards, including surprise factory inspections. As a result, the famous UL seal everywhere inspires consumer confidence.[23]

Private certification in the service industries is similar to that in the product industries. For example, the Best Western company doesn't own and operate motels. Rather, it lets motel owners display the Best Western name and link to its computerized reservation service if they satisfy its criteria for quality and comfort. The Best Western sign tells potential guests that they can count on a certain level of service. Like all brand names, this service saves people the risk that accompanies unfamiliarity and thus allows them to economize their time.[24]

Similar functions are performed by a spectrum of private organizations, ranging from the American Automobile Association to insurance companies that promote safety.[25] The potential for private certification is as broad as the marketplace itself. For example, certification companies could easily take the place of government licensing agencies in medicine, law, and other professions. In all such cases, government restrictions were enacted not at the bidding of consumers for their own protection but rather at the bidding of the practitioners for the protection of their own incomes from growing competition.[26]

Today we cannot know what private consumer protection would look like were government to exit the field. As the Austrian school of economics teaches, the competitive process and the lure of profit encourage people to discover things that won't be discovered otherwise. When the market for consumer protection is liberated from the stultifying hand of government, new ways of protecting consumers will proliferate.

Related to the fear of uncertainty is the fear of what is called atomism. This is the concern that in the unfettered marketplace of individualists, with no government safety net, too many people will be left to fall by the wayside. In 1997, President Clinton tempered his declaration that the era of big government was over by adding that we couldn't go back to the time when "people fended for themselves."[27] Juxtaposing the two points implied that big government was established so that people wouldn't have to fend for themselves. Clinton undoubtedly had in mind the second definition of the term "fend" in the *American Heritage Dictionary,* third edition: "to attempt to manage without assistance." The word also suggests that favorite phrase of capitalism's enemies, "the survival of the fittest." The two terms are related — and equally misused.

If to fend is to attempt to manage without assistance, it has little relevance to the free market. The marketplace is characterized by the division of labor and exchange for mutual benefit: you make shoes, I'll make bread, and we'll trade. Does that sound like fending for oneself? It sounds more like mutual assistance and cooperation. One becomes suspicious of capitalism's enemies when their model of an individualist resembles Theodore Kaczynski, who was hostile to everything associated with capitalism.

But what about the anticapitalist's worst bogey, competition? Isn't it properly described as "dog eat dog"? Wrong. As noted, free cooperation breeds competition. Competition is what happens when people are free to decide with whom they will cooperate. The alternative is forced cooperation with whomever the state selects.

Man being a social animal, there most likely was never a time when individuals literally fended for themselves. They always lived in groups and lived by reciprocity. The conjured-up era of fending is simply part of the anti-capitalist folklore designed to make us fear liberty and look to the state for protection. Atomistic individualism is a straw man. It was never part of the classical liberal, or libertarian, picture of the world. That world is better described as embodying "molecular individualism."

It is true, of course, that in a free society, someone needing assistance can't compel others to come to his rescue. But as argued in chapter 5, compulsion is not necessary.

Let's now look at that phrase "the survival of the fittest." How ironic! At the advent of industrial capitalism the earth could barely support a billion people. Life expectancy was not much more than thirty years. Today about six billion people are living longer, healthier lives than ever before. (The exceptions are the result of civil wars and statist social systems.) Global life expectancy is about sixty-four years. In the most advanced countries, of course, it is considerably longer.[28] As Julian Simon has so eloquently shown, material welfare in every category — from food production per capita to leisure time — is booming.[29]

It is also worth pointing out that capitalism, at worst, embodies the principle "the *advancement* (not survival) of the fittest." The producers who are most successful, that is, most responsive to consumers, get rich. But the losers don't get killed. They merely go out of business. The less productive don't die; they simply make lower incomes, which as we saw in chapter 5, are worth more and more all the time.

Finally, the welfare state (like socialism) doesn't abolish the "survival of the fittest" principle; it merely redefines what it means to be fit. Under statism, the fit are those who are best at navigating the bureaucratic rivers and rivulets. Those who are most sophisticated in the ways of legislatures and government agencies (the poor are not among them) get most of the rewards.

The upshot is that the system that allegedly permits only the "fit" to survive seems also best at making more people increasingly fit. Sounds like a good deal.

Well-intentioned people have also advocated the welfare state out of a sense of "social justice." They feel that the gap between rich and poor, the alleged power disparity between employer and employee, or any number of other things, is unfair. There are two answers here. First, as F. A. Hayek pointed out, justice is an attribute of willed conduct, and so it is illegitimate to attach the term or its antipode to impersonal processes, such as the marketplace, in which "the resulting state was not the intended aim of the individual actions."[30] No one willed the configuration of incomes in a free market; it is the result of countless actions and transactions by individuals who had anything on their minds *but* the distribution of incomes. No one *decided* that Bill Gates would be a multibillionaire.

We didn't decide this even as a society. Instead, lots of people simply bought his products, the unintended consequence of which was Gates's fortune. Society and the market are abstractions denoting particular kinds of transactions among individuals. They have no independent existence and do not act or make decisions, despite what John Stuart Mill implied when he said that "society should treat all equally well who have deserved equally well of it."[31] If individuals acted justly in each transaction, there is no cause for calling the unintended overall result unjust. Violating the rights of individuals in the name of social justice through, say, forced "redistribution" is a contradiction in terms. If you want justice, social or otherwise, work for freedom.[32]

Second, since government intervention hampers the production of wealth, it is an odd way to achieve any reasonable objective labeled "social justice."[33] Would the advocate of social justice truly prefer that we be more nearly "equal" at a lower standard of living? Or might it not be preferable for everyone to be getting richer even if the gap between the top and bottom grows?

Thus we see that government is not needed to perform the functions considered the province of the welfare state. Charity, insurance, consumer protection, and the other services provided by coercive government can be, and at one time or another have been, offered by entrepreneurs in the free market. Indeed, the services were undoubtedly superior, considering that they were untainted by compulsion, favor-seeking, and political deception. A bureaucracy is never as competent at delivering the goods as an enterprise. How could it be? A bureaucracy has a guaranteed clientele and flow of revenue (taxes).[34] An enterprise has to attract willing customers. It can't take you for granted the way a bureaucracy does. Moreover, bureaucracy by nature is cut off from the discovery process that is generated by the free actions of people in the competitive/cooperative marketplace. An enterprise is a participant in that process; entrepreneurs lured by the prospect of profit are ever alert to new, hitherto unnoticed opportunities to please customers. When bureaucracy replaces enterprise, we literally do not know what we are missing.[35]

We saw in chapter 4 that a group of American intellectuals systematically promoted collectivist ideas in order to change the direction of the country. They did this for good and bad motives, but they did it all the same. (Bad motive: grubby businessmen make more money than I, a lofty, sensitive intellectual, do; something should be done about that.) They made a moral appeal that found wide acceptance. In my view, this is one of the keys to understanding the change in America.

The American Revolution was a remarkable event in world history, with roots in antiquity, the Middle Ages, the Renaissance, and the French and Scottish Enlightenments. Obviously, I don't speak here of the military conflict with England, but of the preceding intellectual revolution, the one in which Thomas Paine hurled written salvos at the enemy: tyranny, monarchy, and collectivism. That revolution marked a change in thinking about politics and economics. The divine right of kings was deposed. Mercantilism, if not dismantled, was reined in. Government was limited.

But a philosophical and, specifically, moral revolution did not accompany the political revolution, which was left incomplete.

Capitalism is the political economy of rational self-interest. It is based on each person's right to decide what he wants in life and then to strive to achieve it; Ayn Rand calls this the right to live for one's own sake.[36] No person is burdened by law with an unchosen obligation to look after others. Each is free to make his own well-being his life's cause.

That undeniable characteristic of capitalism has always made people uncomfortable because it clashes with moral teachings received from an early age condemning self-interest ("selfishness") as wicked. Those who indicted capitalism in the nineteenth century nearly always did so for its encouragement of acquisitiveness and selfishness, which were equated with the desire to liberate oneself from the drudgery and physical labor of the precapitalist era. Bernard Bosanquet, who was regarded as a liberal, favored "moral socialism," which exposed the evil of "egoism, materialism, and Epicureanism" while making the public good part of the "moral essence of the individual."[37] We hear such indictments to this day. For example: "The moral appeal of socialism and state intervention," write Daniel Yergin and Joseph Stanislaw, "is clear and explicit: altruism, sympathy and solidarity with fellow human beings; dignity and social betterment; justice and fairness. The market system's moral basis is more subtle and indirect."[38]

As long as self-interest is regarded as evil, or at least highly suspect, laissez faire will not be complete. To the extent that individuals are thought to owe service to society, many people will be sympathetic to government intervention designed to extract that service. To their credit, the Enlightenment thinkers, such as Adam Smith, saw that self-interest did not need to conflict with the good of others, that there is fundamental harmony of interests among

126

people. But they did not wholly escape from the prevailing moral sentiment. They often spoke in terms suggested by Bernard Mandeville's subtitle "private vices, publick virtues," suggesting that self-interest can be permitted only because it serves the public good.[39]

Logically, one can believe in the duty of altruism and still favor laissez faire on the grounds that only *voluntary* service to others is virtuous.[40] But it is unlikely that most people who subscribe to the doctrine of self-sacrifice will be content to leave the discharge of that "obligation" to individual discretion. They will continually be tempted by proposals that promise to align legal obligations with (what they see as) moral obligations, that is, by measures that compel service through the political system. They will not grasp the damage caused by intervention sufficiently to withstand the moral appeal of putting the "public good" first. They will be disarmed by the force of a pseudo-moral argument because it embraces their moral premises.

We should not be surprised that the leading figures in the Republican Party never challenge the foundation of the welfare state. No wonder the vaunted Republican revolution of 1995 was a mirage. Although they declare themselves opponents of big government, Republicans have long accepted such entrenched welfare state programs as Social Security, Medicare, unemployment insurance, and the minimum wage. When Newt Gingrich, leader of the GOP takeover of Congress, retired, he said he would devote his life to saving Social Security, the crown jewel of the American welfare state. This is just "politics."

The welfare state reflects their moral outlook far more faithfully than laissez-faire capitalism does. Top Republicans often defend welfare state measures even when criticizing the welfare state per se. For example, Gingrich, well before his retirement as House Speaker, wrote, "I have argued consistently that Social Security must be off the table in any discussion of a balanced budget. Social Security is the most widely accepted government contract [sic] in America."[41] He hints that a "safer retirement for future generations"[42] could be discussed after the federal budget is balanced, yet he titles a chapter in his book "Balancing the Budget and *Saving* Social Security and Medicare."[43] Gingrich also bragged that the Republicans increased spending on other social programs, including school lunches.[44] To him, a "stunning suggestion for transforming welfare" is to let taxpayers check a box on their tax return in order to divert $100 from the U.S. Treasury to their favorite charity; their own family, no doubt, would not qualify.[45] Indicative also is his statement that Franklin Roosevelt was "probably the greatest President of the twentieth century."[46]

Of course, Gingrich and all Republican leaders support two major welfare state pillars: "public" education, which they would strengthen through national standards and federal vouchers, and the war on drugs, which exists ostensibly to protect the welfare of actual and potential drug users.[47] In education, acceptance of the welfare state premise is palpable. Conservatives support vouchers, among other reasons, on grounds that poor people deserve the same choices in education (but not, presumably, in food and homes) as wealthier people. William J. Bennett, former secretary of education and drug czar in Republican administrations, writes, "There is another issue associated with school choice as well — social justice. At present our most affluent families do exercise choice, by buying a home in the neighborhood of their choice, or by sending their children to a private school. The poor do not now have that kind of choice."[48] How are they to be given that choice? By the creation of a new entitlement — the voucher — financed by the taxpayers and inevitably accompanied by regulations for schools that seek eligibility to accept them. Thus, the conservative welfare state.

Major conservative spokesmen are clearly uneasy with individualism, despite their occasional limited rhetorical support. By capriciously equating it with libertinism, relativism, or disregard for the rights of others, they see it as destructive of the social order. Conservatives sometimes indict "liberals," the misnomer for the open welfare state advocates, for being overconcerned with the individual. Robert Bork, who ranks second behind Bennett as the conservative vicar of virtue, identifies "radical individualism" — "the drastic reduction of limits to personal gratification" — as an element of what he calls modern liberalism. For Bork, individualism unfettered by "opposing forces" such as morality is a major cause of American decline.[49] Thus does Bork set morality against individualism, conceding morality to the collectivists and undermining the social process, capitalism, that is based on individual rights. Even though he, like Bennett, goes on to say that government cannot be the primary agent in reviving the American culture, their view of individualism can only strengthen the forces of statism. Neither of these thinkers, nor other leading conservative intellectuals, would disagree that service to others is man's primary moral duty. Bennett has complained that the American people are increasingly self-regarding and that "many of us act as if we have reduced the entire Declaration of Independence to a single phrase, 'the pursuit of happiness.'"[50]

Ayn Rand saw in the Jefferson-Locke phrase "life, liberty, and the pursuit of happiness" an implicit moral philosophy of rational self-interest, a philosophy that clashed with the culture's explicit ethics of self-sacrifice. That clash seems hard to deny. Consider that Benjamin Rush signed the Declaration of Independence and also said, when promoting government schooling, "Let our pupil be taught that he does not belong to himself, but that he is public property. Let him be taught to love his family, but let him be taught at the same time that he must forsake and even forget them when the welfare of his country requires it."[51] One cannot be a self-owner and property of the state at the same time.

"That which is merely implicit," such as a moral principle, Rand commented, "is not in men's conscious control; they can lose it by means of other implications, without knowing what it is that they are losing or when or why. It was the morality of altruism that undercut America."[52] To fight for capitalism, she added, one must openly promote the morality of rational self-interest.

Confusion abounds about the issues of self-interest, altruism, and capitalism. Writers such as George Gilder have argued that capitalism is based on self-sacrifice because entrepreneurs earn profits only by serving, attending to the needs of, others.[53] But that is an equivocation over the word "serve." A waitress can be a rational egoist, although she certainly serves others. To hold otherwise is to conflate the moral and the economic senses of "service."

Of course, an entrepreneur earns profits by offering consumers something they are willing to pay for. But he does not need to be an altruist to be a good entrepreneur. The quest for personal profit leads him to attend efficiently to others. Adam Smith famously pointed out that it is not from self-sacrifice that the brewer, butcher, and baker provide our dinner, but from their self-interest. (Smith used the term "benevolence" for self-sacrifice, a confusion that exists to this day.[54]) "We address ourselves, not to their humanity," wrote Smith, "but to their self-love, and never talk to them of our own necessities but of their advantages."[55] Indeed, he added that we as consumers would not be nearly as well served if merchants put their own interests aside. "By pursuing his own interest he [the individual] frequently promotes that of society more effectually than when he really intends to promote it. I have never known much good done by those who affected to trade for the publick good."[56]

In respect of Gilder's argument, it matters *why* an entrepreneur serves consumers. If he does so out of a conviction that service is his duty and justification for living, then he is an altruist. But another entrepreneur could perform identical activities out of conviction that his highest moral objective is his own happiness and that trading with others (which requires attention to their wants and needs) is the path to achieving that objective.

The upshot is that capitalism protects the right of people to pursue their self-interest and thus cannot be "based on" altruism. It is socialism that is based on altruism, for it attempts to outlaw self-interest.

If the welfare state is the system that forcibly transfers resources from one to another, tethering citizens and corrupting their independence, its antipode is the free market, or the system of private property. If subsidy tethers, property liberates.

It is hard to overstate how radical the idea of private property is. Although private property was a feature of human life from the earliest times, as a formal principle of law, it dramatically transformed society. According to the Scottish Enlightenment writer Adam Ferguson, man ceased to be a savage when the idea of property occurred to him.[57] The economic blessings yielded by private property have been written about at length. Ludwig von Mises has shown that without property in the means of production, there is no trade; that without trade, there are no prices; and that without prices there can be no economic calculation, which is indispensable for determining how to get the most value from resources. Thus, central planning is impossible, and property rights are required for people to prosper.[58]

Mises and others have defended the role private property plays in providing the incentives for productivity. People who are confident that the fruits of their labor are secure will labor and invest to produce that fruit. Society becomes rich as a result.

Property may be said to have noneconomic implications as well. The relationships between property and liberty and between property and autonomy are particularly relevant. Although the opponents of private property have rhapsodized about freedom, it is difficult to know what they mean. What would freedom without property rights look like? No one has bothered to answer that question. To take one example: critics of property rights often claim to be champions of free speech and free press. Yet how free can speech and press be when private property is not recognized? Where government licenses the press and controls the ink and newsprint, freedom of the press is impossible to envision.

Similarly, enemies of property have advocated personal autonomy and self-determination. Yet how can those things be real-

ized without private property? In a world of collective property —
which in fact would mean state-controlled property — everyone is
a tenant and employee at the mercy of a single landlord and employer. That condition describes the opposite of what we think of as
autonomy; it's serfdom. It is true that in a market society, many people
are both tenants and employees. The difference is that in a market,
there are multiple landlords and employers competing to attract tenants and employees to do business with them. Even the property-
less multitude find that the businessmen are trying to please them.
Moreover, every tenant and employee has the freedom to work to
become a homeowner and an independent entrepreneur.

Property makes serfs freemen and compels would-be rulers to
please consumers. As Mises wrote:

> While under precapitalist conditions superior men were the
> masters on whom the masses of the inferior had to attend, un-
> der capitalism the more gifted and more able have no means to
> profit from their superiority other than to serve to the best of
> their abilities the wishes of the majority of the less gifted.[59]

F. A. Hayek noted that private property creates an "assured
free sphere" for each person, even those who own little.

> The system of private property is the most important guaranty
> of freedom, not only for those who own property, but scarcely
> less for those who do not. It is only because the control of the
> means of production is divided among many people acting
> independently that nobody has complete power over us, that
> we as individuals can decide what to do with ourselves. If all
> the means of production were vested in a single hand, whether
> it be that of "society" as a whole or that of a dictator, whoever
> exercises this control has complete power over us.[60]

Property has made civilization possible. At the dawn of the
human race things must have looked bleak. After all, people need
basically the same things to survive: food, clothing, shelter. But at
any given moment, resources are scarce. That sounds like a recipe
for the Hobbesian war of all against all. But it didn't work out that
way. How can that be? As Mises explained, it was precisely the conditions that could have brought about perpetual war that led instead to peace, cooperation, and prosperity.

131

Because many people or even all people want bread, clothes, shoes, and cars, large-scale production of these goods becomes feasible and reduces the costs of production to such an extent that they are accessible at low prices. The fact that my fellow man wants to acquire shoes as I do, does not make it harder for me to get shoes, but easier.[61]

Freedom, autonomy, dignity, and prosperity depend on private property. To the extent it is violated, civilization is undermined.[62]

But must we go to extremes? it will be asked by some. Sure, they will continue, socialism is bad and unworkable. But a complete free market — laissez faire — cannot be the only alternative. Isn't there a third way?

George Washington said, "Government is not reason, it is not eloquence — it is force!" Every activity it undertakes ultimately relies on coercion. Government does not produce or create; it appropriates and transfers what others produce and create.

In contrast, the marketplace *is* reason and eloquence arising in an environment in which people are free to better their circumstances by offering to better the circumstances of others. The marketplace is creative. Think about what happens there. A successful entrepreneur transforms existing factors — labor, machines, land, raw materials — into something for which people are willing to pay more than they would pay for the separate parts. The entrepreneur creates value.

State and market, then, are opposites, embodying, respectively, force and creativity. That is why the search for a third way is misconceived. There can be no such thing. This is not to deny the possibility of a mixed economy that combines some freedom with some coercion. The point is that any given encounter between individuals, including government officials, is based either on freedom or on coercion. We live in the digital age, in which powerful devices accomplish their wonders through electronic switches that have only two positions: on or off. There is no middle position. It is time we brought our political thinking into the digital age.

The seekers of a third way should be chastened by the fact that several decades ago many people thought the third way between capitalism and Marxist socialism had been found. They even had a name for it. It was called fascism.

The solution to the imposition of the welfare state should be clear. Nothing short of abolition will cut the tethers, free the people to reestablish their independence, and liberate the market to achieve its full potential. The programs of the welfare state should be dismantled in their entirety and the money financing them left in the pockets of the taxpayers. Social Security, Medicare, Medicaid, unemployment insurance, workman's compensation, welfare, public schools, business and farm subsidies, the Earned Income Tax Credit, student loans, aid to the arts and humanities, racial preferences, public broadcasting, rent control, minimum-wage law, compulsory unions, foreign aid (welfare for foreign citizens *and* domestic businesses) — there is no reason for any of them to survive even another day. As an earlier group of abolitionists said, gradualism in theory is perpetuity in practice.

With hundreds of billions of dollars left with America's productive citizens, we would see an explosion of investment that would lift the living standards of everyone. Moreover, since freer and richer Americans will be more benevolent and generous than their poorer and more burdened counterparts, we can expect to see a dramatic expansion of charitable contributions to help the few people who literally cannot care for themselves.[63]

Those who have been made dependent on government will find assistance through voluntary charity and from family and friends. Those who are capable of working will find work. It strains credulity to assert that a free people won't be generous toward those who warrant generosity.

Morally speaking, there is no justification for continuing the institutionalized theft that constitutes the welfare state's forced transfer. The need of, say, a Social Security recipient is no argument for stealing a wage earner's money. Defenders of the welfare state speak of solemn promises and contracts, all of which obscures this fact: *A* cannot legitimately promise *B* that *C* will support him. *C* has a right to liberty. If *B* has a grievance, it is with *A*.

Most important, abolition of the welfare state will remove the tethers that prevent individuals from living completely human lives, for human beings survive and prosper essentially through reason, and for reason to function in its fullness, human beings must be free from aggressive force (and fraud). This in the end is a matter of morality. Morality is about value and virtue, and as Ayn Rand wrote, "It is only the concept of 'Life' that makes the concept of 'Value' possible."[64] The moral is that which makes the rational life possible. The moral *is* the practical. That is no happy coincidence. It is the nature of reality.

Therefore, abolition of the welfare state is eminently moral *and* practical. We can take care of ourselves, untethered, through voluntary association for mutual benefit. Anything less only diminishes us as human beings.

Why abolition? Because, as Henry David Thoreau said in "Civil Disobedience," "This government never furthered any enterprise but by the alacrity with which it got out of the way."

Abolish the welfare state; remove the tethers — and watch man soar.

Notes

¹ See Sheldon Richman, *Your Money or Your Life: Why We Must Abolish the Income Tax* (Fairfax, Va.: The Future of Freedom Foundation, 1999).

² See Ayn Rand, "Appendix: Man's Rights," in her *Capitalism: The Unknown Ideal* (New York: Signet Books, 1967), pp. 320–28.

³ See Thomas Szasz, *Fatal Freedom: The Ethics and Politics of Suicide* (Westport, Conn.: Praeger, 1999), pp. 64–66, 68–71, 76–86, and 104.

⁴ Bertrand de Jouvenel, *The Ethics of Redistribution* (1952; Indianapolis: Liberty Press, 1990), p. 78.

⁵ This is not the place to examine that rationale. Here I merely want to examine whether the welfare state meets the test of a proper function of government according to America's traditions and founding documents. Thomas Jefferson's social-contract theory in the Declaration of Independence, which comes straight from John Locke, has many problems. Those who wish to investigate these issues should consult Murray Rothbard, *For a New Liberty* (New York: Macmillan, 1978) and *The Ethics of Liberty* (New York: New York University Press, 1998).

⁶ The Tenth Amendment, of course, strikes the hammer again when it says that powers not enumerated in the Constitution belong to the people or the states.

⁷ The idea that the free market cannot provide "public goods" is standard fare in economics, but it is flawed. See *Public Goods and Market Failures: A Critical Examination,* ed. Tyler Cowen (New Brunswick, N.J.: Transaction Publishers, 1992). The book contains the classic paper by Ronald Coase showing that, contrary to what public-goods theory predicts, lighthouses were privately owned in England for many years. Jeffrey Rogers Hummel and Don Lavoie, among others, have shown that the "free rider" problem plagues government more egregiously than it does private activities. ("National Defense and the Public-Goods Problem," in *Arms, Politics, and the Economy: Historical and Contemporary Perspectives,* ed. Robert Higgs (New York: Holmes & Meier, 1990), pp. 37–60.

⁸ Richard A. Epstein, *Takings: Private Property and the Power of Eminent Domain* (Cambridge, Mass.: Harvard University Press, 1985), pp. 306–308.

⁹ Dwight Lee ingeniously illustrates this point by imagining what would happen if seconds of people's lives could be "redistrib-

uted." See his essay "The Perversity of Doing Good at Others' Expense," *The Freeman: Ideas on Liberty,* September 1997, pp. 525–28.

[10] H. B. Acton, *The Morals of Markets and Related Essays,* ed. David Gordon and Jeremy Shearmur (Indianapolis: Liberty Fund, 1993), p. 96.

[11] Robert Nozick's "entitlement theory of justice" yields the opposite of the interventionist welfare state. *Anarchy, State, and Utopia* (New York: Basic Books, 1974).

[12] Thomas Szasz's aphorism — in the animal kingdom the rule is eat or be eaten; in the human kingdom it's define or be defined — suggested my own version above.

[13] H. L. Mencken, "A Blind Spot," in *The Vintage Mencken,* ed. Alistair Cooke (New York: Vintage Books, 1955), p. 76.

[14] Helmut Schoeck, *Envy: A Theory of Social Behavior* (1966; Indianapolis: Liberty Press, 1987), p. 234. Schoeck identifies another motive rather influential in politics, the guilty conscience, the flip side of envy.

[15] Jouvenel, p. 78. Schoeck observes that people envy only people like themselves.

[16] Ludwig von Mises, *Human Action: A Treatise on Economics,* 3rd rev. ed. (Chicago: Henry Regnery Company, 1966), p. 852.

[17] Ibid., pp. 269–70. See also Sheldon Richman, "Captain Consumer," *The Freeman: Ideas on Liberty,* February 1999, pp. 38–39.

[18] Mises, *Human Action,* p. 852. On the social function of the freedom to fail, see Dwight R. Lee and Richard B. McKenzie, *Failure and Progress: The Bright Side of the Dismal Science* (Washington, D.C.: Cato Institute, 1993).

[19] See Randall G. Holcombe, *Public Policy and the Quality of Life: Market Incentives versus Government Planning* (Westport, Conn.: Greenwood Press, 1995), pp. 94–106.

[20] Ibid., p. 102.

[21] Milton and Rose Friedman, "Who Protects the Consumer?" in *Free to Choose: A Personal Statement* (New York: Harcourt Brace Jovanovich, 1990), pp. 189–227.

[22] See Daniel B. Klein, *Reputation: Studies in the Voluntary Elicitation of Good Conduct* (Ann Arbor, Mich.: University of Michigan Press, 1997).

[23] Holcombe, pp. 98–99.

²⁴ Ibid., pp. 96–97. Those who dislike national chains because they allegedly erode local character should understand that many travelers prefer the familiarity and assurance of, say, McDonald's to the "character" of Joe's Diner. Even locals seem to like the lower prices at Wal-Mart.

²⁵ Holcombe, pp. 99–101.

²⁶ See Milton Friedman, *Capitalism and Freedom* (Chicago: University of Chicago Press, 1961); also Holcombe, pp. 107–21.

²⁷ Of course, he didn't really mean the era of big government was over; he went on to propose new government spending in the next three years.

²⁸ Nicholas Eberstadt, "Population, Food, and Income: Global Trends in the Twentieth Century," in *The True State of the Planet*, ed. Ronald Bailey (New York: The Free Press, 1995), p. 21. Also important is Nathan Rosenberg and L. E. Birdzell Jr., *How the West Grew Rich: The Economic Transformation of the Industrial World* (New York: Basic Books, 1986).

²⁹ Julian L. Simon, ed., *The State of Humanity* (Cambridge, Mass.: Blackwell Publishers, 1995). See also Simon, *The Ultimate Resource 2* (Princeton, N.J.: Princeton University Press, 1997).

³⁰ F. A. Hayek, *Law, Legislation, Liberty,* vol. 2, *The Mirage of Social Justice* (Chicago: University of Chicago Press, 1976), p. 33.

³¹ Quoted in ibid., p. 63.

³² Robert Nozick has a slightly different take from Hayek's. He calls an unintended result *just* if the initial property holdings and subsequent transactions were just. I don't regard this as a significant difference with Hayek. See Nozick, pp. 150–74. Incidentally, since in the marketplace there is no distribution of income analogous to a distribution of allowances by parents to children, there can be no redistribution. The government schemes are best described as distributive rather than as redistributive.

³³ Mises, *Human Action,* pp. 804–809, 853–54.

³⁴ For a detailed look at how private organizations can perform whatever valuable functions are performed by government regulators, see *Instead of Regulation: Alternatives to Regulatory Agencies,* ed. Robert W. Poole Jr. (Lexington, Mass.: Lexington Books, 1982).

³⁵ See Israel M. Kirzner, *Competition and Entrepreneurship* (Chicago: University of Chicago Press, 1973) and *Perception, Opportunity, and Profit* (Chicago: University of Chicago Press, 1979).

³⁶ Rand, "What Is Capitalism" in *Capitalism: The Unknown*

Ideal, pp. 11–34.

[37] Quoted in Gertrude Himmelfarb, *Poverty and Compassion: The Moral Imagination of the Late Victorians* (New York: Alfred A. Knopf, 1991), p. 315. Chapter 5 of the present book presented other denunciations of capitalism for its foundation on selfishness.

[38] Daniel Yergin and Joseph Stanislaw, "Triumph of the Market: Capitalism Reigns, But Can It Avoid the Excesses of the Past?" *Washington Post,* February 1, 1998, p. C5. (We will see below that equating that list of values with altruism is erroneous.)

[39] Bernard Mandeville, *The Fable of the Bees or Private Vices, Publick Benefits* (1714; Indianapolis: Liberty Classics, 1988).

[40] "The basic principle of altruism is that man has no right to exist for his own sake, that service to others is the only justification for his existence, and that self-sacrifice is his highest moral duty, virtue and value." Ayn Rand, "Faith and Force: The Destroyers of the Modern World," in her *Philosophy: Who Needs It* (New York: Signet, 1982), p. 61.

[41] Newt Gingrich, *To Renew America* (New York: HarperCollins Publishers, 1995), p. 97.

[42] Ibid.

[43] Emphasis added. During President Clinton's 1998 State of the Union address, Gingrich heartily applauded Clinton's command to Congress to "save Social Security first." Gingrich sat on his hands at other points in the speech.

[44] Ibid., p. 98.

[45] Ibid., p. 76.

[46] Ibid., p. 36. Ronald Reagan was another admirer of Roosevelt.

[47] See William J. Bennett, *Devaluing America: The Fight for Our Culture and Our Children* (New York: Summit Books, 1992). Bennett praises the early movement to establish public, or common, schools. "The advocates of the common school felt that a nation could fulfill its destiny only if every new generation was taught these values together in a common institution" (pp. 57–58).

[48] Ibid., p. 65.

[49] Robert H. Bork, *Slouching towards Gomorrah: Modern Liberalism and American Decline* (New York: Regan Books, 1996), pp. 5–8, 332. The other major cause is radical egalitarianism. Bork acknowledges the tension between individualism and egalitarianism.

[50] William Bennett, "The National Prospect," *Commentary,* November 1995, p. 30. See also Bennett, *The Index of Leading Cultural Indicators* (Washington, D.C.: Empower America, Heritage Foundation, Free Congress Foundation, 1993). My thanks to Robert Bidinotto of the Institute for Objectivist Studies for bringing this point to my attention. See Bidinotto, "The GOP's Foreign Imports," *IOS Journal,* April-June 1996.

[51] Quoted in Joel Spring, *The American School: 1642–1985* (New York: Longman, 1985), p. 34. Rush also said the student "must be taught to amass wealth, but it must be only to increase his power of contribution to the wants and needs of the state" (ibid.).

[52] See Ayn Rand, *For the New Intellectual* (New York: Signet Books, 1961), p. 53. See also "What Is Capitalism?" Rand links the flaws in moral philosophy to the corruption of reason.

[53] George Gilder, *Wealth and Poverty* (New York: Basic Books, 1981).

[54] David Kelley has given this confusion close attention and has admirably sorted it out in *Unrugged Individualism: The Selfish Basis of Benevolence* (Poughkeepsie, N.Y.: Institute for Objectivist Studies, 1996).

[55] Adam Smith, *An Inquiry into the Nature and Causes of the Wealth of Nations,* book 1, chapter 2, (1776; Indianapolis: Liberty Press, 1981), pp. 26–27.

[56] Ibid., book 4, chapter 2, p. 456.

[57] See the discussion in F. A. Hayek, *The Fatal Conceit: The Errors of Socialism* (Chicago: University of Chicago Press, 1988), p. 35.

[58] Mises's argument and other papers on the calculation problem are found in *Collectivist Economic Planning: Critical Studies on the Possibilities of Socialism,* ed. F. A. Hayek (1935; Clifton, N.J.: Augustus M. Kelley, 1975).

[59] Ludwig von Mises, "On Equality and Inequality," in *The Libertarian Reader,* ed. David Boaz (New York: Free Press, 1997), p. 106.

[60] F. A. Hayek, *The Road to Serfdom* (Chicago: University of Chicago Press, 1944), pp. 103–104.

[61] Mises, *Human Action,* p. 673.

[62] See Tom Bethell, *The Noblest Triumph: Property and Prosperity through the Ages* (New York: St. Martin's Press, 1998) for a

comprehensive look at the role of private property in human well-being.

[63] There is no conflict between self-interested individualism and generosity toward people in unfortunate circumstances through no fault of their own — quite the contrary. See Kelley.

[64] Ayn Rand, "The Objectivist Ethics," in *The Virtue of Selfishness: A New Concept of Egoism* (New York: Signet, 1964), pp. 15–16.

About the Author

Sheldon Richman is senior fellow at The Future of Freedom Foundation in Fairfax, Virginia, and the editor of *Ideas on Liberty,* published by The Foundation for Economic Education, Irvington-on-Hudson, New York. His first book, *Separating School & State: How to Liberate America's Families,* was published by The Future of Freedom Foundation in 1994. He formerly was senior editor at the Cato Institute and the Institute for Humane Studies at George Mason University.

Richman has written widely on a variety of topics, including education, population and the environment, taxation, federal disaster policy, international trade, the Second Amendment, and American history. His work has appeared in the *Washington Post*; *Wall Street Journal*; *USA Today*; *Washington Times*; *Chicago Tribune*; *Christian Science Monitor*; *San Francisco Chronicle*; *Detroit News*; *American Scholar*; *Journal of Economic Growth*; *Education Week*; *Regulation*; *The World and I*; *Insight*; *The Freeman: Ideas on Liberty*; *Reason*; and *Liberty*.

He is a contributor to *The Fortune Encyclopedia of Economics.*

Richman has appeared on CNN's *Crossfire* and *Both Sides* with Jesse Jackson; CNBC's *Business Insiders*; ABC's *This Week with David Brinkley*; the *Montel Williams Show*; and radio programs across the United States.

He is formerly a newspaper reporter and magazine editor and was graduated from Temple University in his hometown, Philadelphia. He has three children, who are home-schooled.

About the Publisher

Founded in 1989, The Future of Freedom Foundation is a 501(c)(3), tax-exempt, educational foundation that presents an uncompromising moral, philosophical, and economic case for individual freedom, private property, and limited government.

The officers of The Foundation are: Jacob G. Hornberger (Fairfax, Virginia), president, and Richard M. Ebeling (Hillsdale, Michigan), vice president of academic affairs. There are seven members on The Foundation's board of trustees. *Freedom Daily* is published monthly by The Foundation. It consists of essays, book reviews, and quotations from freedom's greatest champions. Subscribers come from thirty countries. The price of a one-year subscription is $18 ($25 foreign). The Foundation also shares its ideas on liberty with others through lectures, speeches, seminars, radio appearances, and its web page, www.fff.org.

The Foundation neither solicits nor accepts governmental funds. Operations are financed through subscription revenues and donations, which are invited in any amount. Please contact us for additional information.

The Future of Freedom Foundation
11350 Random Hills Road, Suite 800
Fairfax, Virginia 22030
(703) 934-6101
Fax (703) 352-8678
email: fff@fff.org
www.fff.org

Index

A

Acton, John Emerich Edward
Dalberg, Lord, 46
Adams, Charles Francis Jr., 69–70,
72
Aid to Dependent Children (ADC):
becomes Aid to Families with
Dependent Children (AFDC), 37,
100; effect of program, 107
Albert, Carl B., 18
Alm, Richard, 95–96
Altruism: basic principle of (Rand),
138 (n40); as basis for socialism,
126–30; morality of, 129
Armour, J. Ogden, 39
Arrears Act (1879), 71
Austrian school of economics, 123

B

Baldwin, Roger, 73
Barkai, Avraham, 56
Bastiat, Frédéric, ix, 17, 30, 34
Batten, Samuel Zane, 70
Beck, Hermann, 53, 55
Beito, David T., 107
Bellamy, Edward, 72–79, 84
Bellows, Henry W., 70–71
Bennett, William J., 128
Bismarck, Otto von, xvii–xviii, 40–
41; connection to Nazism, 55;
philosophy of state socialism,
47–52; social-welfare programs
of, 47; use of idea of welfare
state, xi, xvii–xviii, 79
Bono, Sonny, 38
Bork, Robert, 24, 128
Bosanquet, Bernard, 126
Bourne, Randolph, 82
Brennan, Geoffrey, 29
Brooks, John Graham, 72
Brownson, Orestes, 69

C

Campaign finance system, 34
Capitalism: Bellamy's criticism of,
74; promotion of, 129; self-
interest under, 126, 130; social
mobility under, 119; welfare state
predates, xv
Charitable organizations, private:
in nineteenth-century Britain,
xvii; private donations to, 105; as
safety net, xii, 104–105
Choice: absent in Bellamy's collectivism, 78–79; collective, 26–27;
in the marketplace, 26–30; political, 26–29. See also Electoral
vote
Churchill, Winston, 46–47
Cleveland, Grover, 71
Clinton, Hillary Rodham, 91
Clinton, William Jefferson, 1, 105,
117, 123
Clinton administration: downsizing of government during, 40;
welfare legislation of, 37–38
Collectivism: criticism of, 58; ex-
periments in and legacy of, xv;
ideas of American intellectuals,
79–80, 125–26; influence of Bellamy's, 72–79. See also Socialism
Collectivization of America, 67–69
Communism, xi, xv; welfare state
distinct from, 16
Competition: absent in Bellamy's
plan, 74–77; importance of, 77–
78; U.S. Postal Service limits, 8
Conservatives: complaints about
welfare, ix–x; as majoritarians, 24
Constitution, U.S.: idea of general
welfare in, 15–16; limits on power of government in, 24; Progressive criticism of, 78; taking of
private property under, 117–18;

145

welfare state incompatible with, xii–xiii

Consumer protection: by competitive market, 120–23; under the welfare state, 5–7, 120

Cooley, Charles H., 79

Costs of welfare state, 1–3

Cox, W. Michael, 95–96

Croly, Herbert, 78, 82, 83, 84

D

Darrow, Clarence, 73

Dawson, W. H., 47–48, 50

Debs, Eugene V., 67

de Jouvenel, Bertrand, 117, 119

Democracy: despotism of (Tocqueville), 10–12; and ignorance, 31–33; idea of collective choice in, 26–27; interest groups in, 32–33; key to, 25; moral problems of, 24–25; as rule of minorities, 33–35

Dependence: of citizens on the German state, 52–54; of citizens on U.S. government, 1, 12; created by antipoverty programs, 100; in nineteenth-century Britain (Fawcett), xvi–xvii; welfare programs foster, xii

Dewey, John, 61 (n16), 73, 74, 82, 83

Disraeli, Benjamin, 46

Douglas, Jack, 15–16

Downs, Anthony, 25–26

Draper, John W., 69

E

Education: government control of, 4, 13; cost of, 2; Republican Party support of public, 128

Eisenach, Eldon, 39, 67, 68, 79, 80

Ekirch, Arthur A. Jr., 67, 73

Electoral vote: choices in, 26–29; concept of majority rule, 25–26; in a democracy, 26–28; logrolling, 30–31, 35, 92–93; paradoxes in, 31–32

Eliot, Charles, 72

Ely, Richard T., 79–80

Emerson, Ralph Waldo, 68

Epstein, Richard, 118

Eyck, Erich, 62 (n28)

F

Fabians, 46

Fascism, xi, xv, 132

Fawcett, Henry, xvi–xvii

Ferguson, Adam, 130

Food and Drug Administration (FDA), 5–6

Founding Fathers: understanding of freedom, xi; understanding of general welfare, 15–16

Frankfurter, Felix, 82

Franklin, Benjamin, 13

Frederickson, George M., 69, 70

Freedom: in Bellamy's collectivism, 78; as key to prosperity, 104; and private property, 130–31

Free riding, 32, 135 (n7)

Friedman, David, 30

Friedman, Milton, 14, 30, 121

Friedman, Rose, 121

Früh, Walter, 55

G

Galbraith, John Kenneth, 47

Gates, Bill, 124–25

Gaullieur, Henry, 57–58

Germany: Historical School in, 47–48; origin of the welfare state in, xvii–xviii; social insurance in, 50–53. *See also* Bismarck, Otto von; Welfare state

Gilder, George, 129

Gingrich, Newt, 127–28

Gladstone, William E., 46

Gore, Al, 92

Government: activist, 14–19, 67–68; as benefactor, 35; control of education, 4, 13; influence on production, 102–104; transfers of wealth in spending of, 2, 117; welfare spending of, 105; welfare state gives power to, 10, 117. *See also* Collectivism

H

Hahn, Adalbert, 55
Hamilton, Alexander, 40, 66
Hardwig, John, 116
Harrison, Lawrence E., 93
Hayek, F. A., 14, 40, 55–56, 77, 80, 124, 131
Hazlitt, Henry, 14, 17, 95
Hentoff, Nat, 116
Herron, George, 70
Higgs, Robert, 81
Himmelfarb, Gertrude, 46, 98–99
Historical School, 47–48
Hitler, Adolf, 55, 56
Hobson, J. A., 99
Holcombe, Randall, 120–21
Holmes, Oliver Wendell Jr., 70
Hughes, Jonathan R. T., 66
Hume, David, 91
Hummel, Jeffrey Rogers, 66

I

Ignorance, rational, 31–33
Individualism: atomistic and molecular, 123–24; conservative view of, 128; radical, 128
Individualism, American: blamed for Civil War, 69; pre–Civil War period, 65, 68; replaced by nationalism, 68–69
Insurance programs: cost of U.S. social, 2–3; of fraternal organizations, 105–107; German state-controlled, 50–53. *See also* Medicare; Social Security
Interest groups: benefits from government regulation, 38–39; bidding and lobbying activities of, 33–35, 92–93; incentives for, 32–33

J

James, William, 70
Jefferson, Thomas, 3–4, 33, 66, 68, 117
Jevons, William Stanley, xvii
Johnson administration, 18

K

Kirzner, Israel, 77
Kolko, Gabriel, 39

L

Labor market: Bellamy's plan for, 75–76; job-training programs, 38; regulation in, 5
Laissez faire: collectivist opponents of, 74; competition in, 77–78; perceived selfishness of, 70; and self-interest, 126
Lamm, Richard, 116
Lassalle, Ferdinand, 54–55
Leoni, Bruno, 25–26
Leuchtenburg, William E., 83
Libertarians: belief about rendering assistance, 101; want repeal of welfare state, x
Lincoln, Abraham, 27, 70
Lippmann, Walter, 82
Lloyd George, David, 46–47
Lobbying, 34–35
Logrolling, 30–31, 35, 92–93
Lomasky, Loren, 29
Looking Backward: 2000–1887 (Bellamy), 72–79

M

Macmillan, Harold, 46
Madison, James, 15–16, 24
Maehl, William Harvey, 52–53
Mandeville, Bernard, 127
Markets: choice in free, 26–30; create security, 120; government interference with, 13–14; provide consumer protection, 120–23
Marx, Karl, 48, 54, 55

McChesney, Fred, 34
Medicare: fiscal unsoundness of, 7;
 government price setting under,
 10; motivation for enactment of,
 18, 36–37
Melville, Herman, 68–69
Mencken, H. L., 33, 119
Mercantilism: effect of American
 intellectual revolution on, 126;
 government control and regulation under, xv, 45–46
Mill, John Stuart, 101, 125
Mises, Ludwig von, 14, 49, 76, 77,
 119–20, 130–32
Mitchell, William, 23, 30, 31
Murray, Charles, 78, 99–100
Mutual-aid organizations: activities of, 106; fraternal insurance
 societies, 105–107; moral component of, 107

N

National Fraternal Congress, 106–
 107
Nationalism: Croly's New National-
 ism, 82; in Germany, 53; post–
 Civil War American, 68–69
National Socialism (Nazism):
 economic ideas in, 56; link to
 welfare state, 55–57
Nevins, Allan, 68
New Deal, 82–84. *See also* Social
 Security
Nozick, Robert, 137 (n32)

P

Paine, Thomas, 126
Parmelee, Maurice, 80
Paternalism: of German-trained
 American intellectuals, 79–80,
 125–26; of government safety net,
 104; of welfare state, 11–14, 57–
 58
Patten, Simon, 77
Payne, James, 38
Pension systems: private plans

compared with Social Security,
 10; for U.S. Civil War veterans,
 34, 71–72. *See also* Social
 Security
Phillips, Wendell, 69
Politicians: actions to get reelected,
 35; deceptive practices of, 35–41;
 responding to interest-group demands, 34–35
Poor laws, English, xvi–xvii, 46
Poor people: gains from economic
 growth, 103–104; in the United
 States, 96–97
Poverty: different measures of, 95–
 97; government definitions of, 95;
 in nineteenth-century Britain,
 xvi–xvii, 46, 98–99; political exploitation of, 91–93; poverty
 line, 95; Radowitz's social-
 kingdom solution to, 54
Powell, John Wesley, 70
Progressive Era: government regulation during, 38–39; growth
 of government during, 81–82;
 idea of collectivism during, 69–
 70; influence of German social
 science on, 79–81; influence of
 Reform Darwinism during, 79;
 political ideology of, 67
Property, private: critics of, 130;
 freedom and incentives with,
 130–31; need for ownership
 (Mises), 76; taking of, 117–18
Property rights: effect of disparaging, 103; government attempts to
 subvert, 9
Protectionism: effect on labor market, 7; as indirect transfer of
 wealth, 17; under state socialism
 in Germany, 50

R

Radowitz, Josef Maria von, 53–54
Rand, Ayn, 126, 129, 133
Rauch, Jonathan, 34–35
Reagan, Ronald, 40

Regulation: deceptive practices of regulators, 35–41; of industry, 38–39; interest-group benefits from, 38–40; interferes with self-regulation, 120–21; meat-inspection program, 38–39; of private-sector activities, 5–9, 38–39, 120–21; of Progressive Era, 81–82

Republican Party: acceptance of welfare state by, 127–28; use of Civil War veterans' pension system, 71

Reynolds, Alan, 94

Richter, Adolf, 55

Rights: under capitalism, 126; counterfeit, 113–15; defined, 94–95; to medical care, 113–17; as moral concept, 115; under U.S. Constitution, 24; welfare rights, 115

Rodbertus, Carl, 54

Roosevelt, Franklin D.: dishonest portrayal of Social Security, 36; on Social Security payroll contributions, 19; welfare state emerges in administration of, ix. *See also* New Deal

Roosevelt, Theodore, 74, 82

Ross, Edward A., 79, 81

Rousseau, Jean Jacques, 80–81

Rush, Benjamin, 129

S

Scalia, Antonin, 24

Schmoller, Gustav, 48

Schoeck, Helmut, 119

Security: free-market creation of, 120; in free society, 14; under welfare state, 13–14

Self-interest: of bureaucrats and politicians, xi–xii; under capitalism, 126–30; criticism of idea of selfishness of, 48, 70; in promotion of capitalism, 129–30; rational, 129

Self-regulation, 120–21

Simmons, Randy, 23, 30, 31

Simon, Julian, 124

Sinclair, Upton, 38, 73

Skocpol, Theda, 71

Smith, Adam, 91, 96, 126, 129

Social Democratic Party (Germany), 52

Social-kingdom concept, 53–54

Social Security: effect on fraternal insurance plans, 107; employer contribution to, 36; fiscal unsoundness of, 7, 9–10; government-determined payroll tax, 9–10; misrepresentation of Medicare under, 36–37; motivation for enactment of, 18–19, 25; Roosevelt's dishonest portrayal of, 36; transfers of wealth under, 16; workers' support of retired workers under, 6–7, 9. *See also* Aid to Dependent Children (ADC); Medicare

Socialism, xv; based on altruism, 126–30; differences between state socialism and, 49; Marxian, 49, 67, redistribution under, xi; Spencer's perception of, 58; in United States, 67; welfare state distinct from, 16. *See also* Collectivism; State socialism

Sowell, Thomas, 100

Spencer, Herbert, 58, 78

Stanislaw, Joseph, 126

State socialism: of Bismarck's Germany, 47–52; social insurance under German, 50–53

Stimson, Henry L., 82

Stolper, Gustav, 56–57

Sumner, William Graham, 78

T

Tanner, Michael, 95, 97, 105

Taxation: as compulsion, 114–15; of income, 4–5; of products and goods, 7; revenues to support

government programs, 107
Taylor, A. J. P., 52
Thoreau, Henry David, 134
Tocqueville, Alexis de, 10–12, 24, 65, 98
Tugwell, Rexford Guy, 83–84
Twentieth Century Fund, 80
Twight, Charlotte, 18

V

Voting. *See* Electoral vote

W

Wagener, Hermann, 53–55
Wagner, Adolf, 48
Walker, Francis A., 69
Ward, Lester F., 79
Washington, George, 132
Wealth: distribution of, 101–103; growth in nineteenth century of, 101
Wealth transfers: deadweight loss in, 30–31; in drug prohibition, 16–17; indirect, 17, 36; motives for, 113; under welfare state, 16–17
Weaver, Richard, 65
Webb, Beatrice, 60 (n7)
Webb, Sidney, 60 (n7)
Welfare: Founders' understanding of general, 15–16; material, 124; size of welfare industry, 38; United States Sanitary Commission as social, 70–71
Welfare programs: Civil War veterans' pension system, 34, 71–72; criticism of, ix–x; current levels of, 38; of Great Society, 100; moral and economic effects of, 12; pre–New Deal state-level, 107; recent reforms in, xviii, 94
Welfare rights: idea of, 94–95; 1960s movement for, 94
Welfare state: abolition of, 132–34; actions that legitimate, 19; advocacy of, 12, 14; apparent benefits

to taxpaying sector, 3; argument to expand, xii; Bismarck's creation of, xi, xvii–xviii; cost of, 1–3; defense of, 23, 133; defined, 16; dependence on, 13–14; dishonesty of, 38–40; distinct from socialism and communism, 16; in England and Great Britain, xv–xvii, 46–47, 95–99; Gaullieur's criticism of, 57–58; government activities of U.S., 4–9; idea of, 14–17; ideology behind, xi; illegitimate, immoral, and unconstitutional, x, 10, 19, 118; incompatibility with constitutional government, xii–xiii; legacy of, 100–101; origin of modern, xvii–xviii; as political choice, 23, 29–30; Republican acceptance of, 127; spending for social-insurance programs of, 2–3; state socialism in Germany, xvii–xviii, 47–55; transfer of resources and wealth under, 3, 16–17, 35, 113, 130, 133; use in United States of idea of, xi–xii. *See also* Dependence; Regulation; Social Security
Welfare state, German: bureaucracy and civil service of, 53; link to Nazism, 55–56; origin of, xvii–xviii. *See also* Bismarck, Otto von; State socialism
Wickard v. Filburn (1941), 13
William I (of Germany), 52
William II (of Germany), xvii
Williams, Walter, 25
Wilson, Woodrow, 82

Y

Yergin, Daniel, 126